CONTENTS

COOK IN SEASON

From THE GOOD COOK

A Different Touch

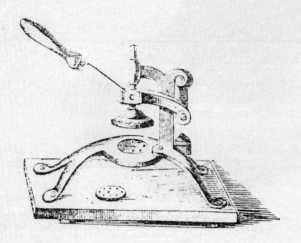

Whether you want to exercise your culinary creativity with a new dish for a dinner party, or simply find something easy but a little different to feed the family, minced meat makes an excellent starting point. It is easy to work with, lends itself equally well to strong or subtle flavourings, and—as prudent cooks have long appreciated—goes further when combined judiciously with other good ingredients. In this volume we show you how to make savoury meatballs (page 7), offer a few interesting variations on the perennially popular hamburger (*pages 20-21*), introduce an exotic Caribbean speciality of baked fruit stuffed with spiced, minced beef (*page 22*) and demonstrate how to make a terrine of aromatic minced pork and vegetables (*page 6*). (The word terrine derives from the earthenware vessel in which it is traditionally cooked: terre, is French for "earth").

For these, and any other, minced meat preparations, the key to success is lean meat of the best quality. Avoid commercially prepared mince, which often contains too much

Perfection in Practice: Lining Terrines

1

Using back fat. Place a slab of chilled back fat rind side down and press one end of the fat against a board to steady it. Using a knife with a long blade, cut across the fat horizontally, working towards the steadying board, to slice off thin sheets of fat.

2

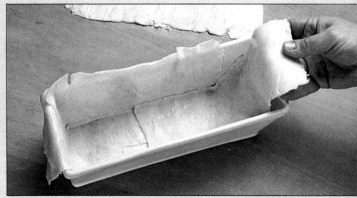

Lining the terrine. Press single sheets of fat against the base, side and ends of the terrine to line it (*above*). Reserve extra sheets to cover the terrine after it has been filled.

fat. Either select the cut of meat you want and ask the butcher to mince it for you, or—even better—mince the meat yourself. You will find that it is well worth spending a little extra time and effort to chop the meat by hand (page 18); its flavour and texture will be far superior to that produced by a meat grinder or processor.

For everyday dishes, such as plain hamburgers, the mince needs only to be seasoned, moulded into patties and briefly fried. You can vary the mixture by adding herbs or enclosing a filling, such as a nugget of Roquefort cheese. For the more elaborate presentation on page 22, the minced meat is first sautéed with garlic, chili peppers and tomatoes to make a spicy stuffing for papaya halves, then baked with a cheese topping just long enough for the fruit to soften and the cheese to acquire a light, golden crust.

Longer cooking—about 1^{1}/$_{2}$ hours — is required for the terrine. To nourish the meat and keep it moist, the terrine is cooked in a dish lined with pork back fat or pieces of lacy caul (below), the fatty membrane from the stomach of the pig. If you cannot obtain fresh caul, your butcher may be able to supply the dry-salted variety, which can be stored for several weeks in a refrigerator or in a freezer. Dry-salted caul, or fresh caul with any stain or odour, should be soaked before use.

The rich, complex flavours of a meat terrine are enhanced and intensified if the dish is allowed to ripen for a few days after it is cooked; covered with plastic film, it may be kept for up to a week in the refrigerator, or in a very cool larder. Because it is not only possible but advisable to prepare it well in advance, a terrine makes an ideal dish for entertaining: serve it as the first course for a dinner party, as part of a buffet, or as the main dish for an informal lunch or supper, with plenty of crusty bread and a bottle of a young, robust red wine.

A terrine mixture can also be used for individual meatballs, known as *caillettes* (*page 7*). Baked in a wrapping of caul, the meatballs acquire an attractively patterned crust. They are delicious served straight from the oven, and even better if kept for a couple of days and served cold.

To follow a richly flavoured starter such as the *caillettes* or a terrine, the main course should be simple — perhaps a plainly roasted game bird, accompanied by a salad (*pages 14-15*). You will need only a light dessert to follow, such as a mellow *crème caramel* (*page 24*).

1 **Using caul.** Soak dry-salted caul in a bowl of tepid water for 15 minutes, to soften it. If the caul has any odour, add a little vinegar or lemon juice to the water; fresh, odourless caul only needs rinsing.

2 **Drying the caul.** After soaking the caul, lift it out of the water. Gently spread it out on a towel to drain off excess moisture.

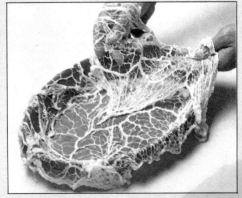

3 **Lining a terrine.** Drape a large piece of caul over the dish. Let it hang over the sides to cover the mixture later. Patch any gaps with smaller pieces of caul.

Rice Croquettes with a Surprise Stuffing

Leftover cooked rice, bound with egg and moulded into a ball round a morsel of stuffing, is quickly transformed by deep frying into a savoury snack or first course. The stuffing can be a tablespoonful of meat sauce (*recipe, page 34*), a chunk of cooked sausage or a slice of soft cheese such as *fontina* or *mozzarella*. In this demonstration, the cooked rice is stuffed with a slice of *mozzarella* cheese and a piece of ham (*recipe, page 34*). The *mozzarella* melts during the brief cooking so that, when the rice croquettes are eaten, the cheese forms the strings that earn this dish its Italian name: *suppli al telefono* or "telephone-wire croquettes".

To ensure that the croquettes will hold together, make them from rice which has been cooked to a clinging consistency. Leftover risotto—round-grain rice cooked with butter, stock and Parmesan cheese and stirred while cooking to give it a moist, creamy consistency (*recipe, page 35*)—is ideal. If possible, make the croquettes with rice that has been refrigerated, well covered, for at least a day; rice is easiest to mould into croquettes when it is quite cold. To provide a crunchy coating, and to prevent the oil from penetrating the croquettes, they are rolled in breadcrumbs before being fried.

Successful deep frying depends on preheating the oil to the right temperature—about 190°C (375°F). If the oil gets too hot, the croquettes will burn; if it is too cool, the oil will penetrate the breadcrumbs before the coating crisps, making the croquettes greasy. To test whether the oil is at the right temperature, throw in a small bread cube and time how long it takes to brown; it should change colour after about 1 minute.

Remember that adding the croquettes will lower the temperature of the oil. To minimize this effect, use a deep pan, with enough oil to submerge the croquettes completely, and cook only a few at a time.

1 **Binding the rice.** Put cold leftover rice in a large bowl. Reserve a handful of the rice on a plate. Add lightly beaten eggs to the bowl; use your hands to mix the eggs gently with the rice (*above*). If necessary, add enough of the reserved rice to make the mixture in the bowl firm.

2 **Cutting up the cheese.** Cut or tear thin slices of ham into small pieces. With a sharp knife, thinly slice some *mozzarella* or similar soft cheese into strips about 2.5 cm (1 inch) long (*above*).

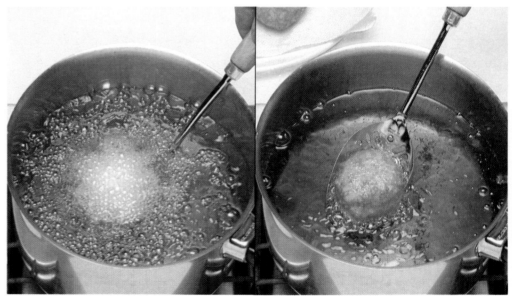

4 **Frying the croquettes.** Pour oil into a large saucepan to a depth of about 7.5 cm (3 inches). Heat the oil to 190°C (375°F). If you have no deep frying thermometer, throw in a bread cube; when the bread cube browns in about 1 minute the oil is ready for cooking. Fry three or four croquettes at a time, using a slotted spoon to lower them into the oil (*above, left*). Fry the croquettes until they are golden-brown—about 1 to 1½ minutes. Lift out the croquettes with the slotted spoon (*above, right*) and drain on absorbent paper.

3 **Forming the croquettes.** Dust your hands with flour. Place a tablespoon of the rice mixture on one hand. Fold a piece of ham and lay it on the rice, then add a slice of cheese (*above, left*) and another tablespoon of rice (*above, centre*). Shape the rice into a ball between your palms (*above, right*). To coat its surface, roll the croquette on a plate of fine breadcrumbs. Firm the croquettes by putting them in the refrigerator for about 30 minutes.

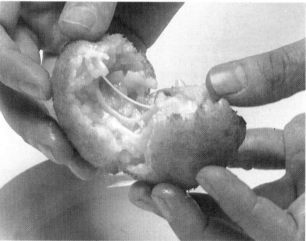

5 **Serving the croquettes.** When all of the croquettes have drained, pile them on a warm dish (*left*) and serve. Eat them with a knife and fork, or with your hands. As you pull apart the two halves of the croquette, the melted cheese will stretch in strings between them (*above*).□

A Simple Meat and Vegetable Terrine

To create a terrine with a uniform texture, any mixture can be cooked in a deep, covered dish—itself known as a terrine—on a rack inside a water bath. The water bath, or bain-marie, is simply a large pan or dish—deep enough to contain the terrine—that is partially filled with boiling water. A water bath can be used in the oven or on top of the stove; for stove-top cooking, cover the pan.

The water that surrounds the terrine will distribute the heat gently and evenly, allowing the entire mixture to cook at the same rate. A covering of foil, or a lid, will prevent any crust from forming on top. As long as the water in the bath comes two-thirds of the way up the sides of the terrine, there is no need to add more water during the cooking period—but if the water level does drop below this point, replenish the bath with boiling water.

Once the terrine is cooked, it may be cooled under weights; this is an effective way of pressing the filling into a cohesive, easily sliced mass. A very heavy weight would, however, force out the terrine's juices and make it dry: for best results, use no more than 1 kg (2 lb) of weights for a 1.25 litre (2 pint) terrine. To distribute the weight evenly, place the weights on a wooden board set on top of the terrine. To prepare a board that can be used again, simply cut a piece of wood to fit inside the rim of the terrine and sand the edges to smooth them. In an emergency, you can substitute cardboard, wrapped in foil to keep it dry; however, it is unlikely to stand up to repeated use.

The terrine on the right is made with a forcemeat based on pork, veal, back fat, pig's liver and chicken livers (*recipe, page 35*), with spinach, celery, onion and herbs providing additional colour and flavour. If you like, you can vary the forcemeat with other leafy vegetables, such as Swiss chard or endive, and finely chopped offal, such as heart, lung or spleen.

As well as providing the filling for a terrine, a forcemeat can be shaped into small balls. A meat and vegetable forcemeat, as here, is traditionally used for the meat balls called *caillettes*. Wrapped in caul and baked uncovered, the *caillettes* will acquire a crusty brown surface (*box, opposite page; recipes, page 36*).

1 **Preparing spinach.** Remove the stems from spinach and wash the leaves well in several changes of water. Bring a large pan of salted water to a rapid boil. Drop the spinach leaves into the water; blanch them for 1 minute. Drain the spinach in a colander and refresh it under cold water. Squeeze the leaves to rid them of excess moisture. Chop the spinach.

2 **Parboiling celery.** Trim the leaves and any damaged or discoloured parts from two or three small sticks of a celery heart. Wash the celery and parboil it in a pan of water until almost tender, about 3 minutes. Remove the celery sticks with a skimmer (*above*). Slice them lengthwise into strips about 5mm (¼ inch) wide; cut the strips crosswise into dice.

5 **Cooking in a water bath.** Cover the terrine with a layer of back fat, folding over any overhanging sheets or adding new sheets as necessary. Cover the terrine with a layer of foil and a lid. Set the terrine on a rack in a larger dish (*above*); place the dish in a preheated 180°C (350°F or Mark 4) oven. Pour in enough boiling water to submerge two-thirds of the terrine. Cook for about 1½ hours. Test for doneness by inserting a thin skewer into the centre of the terrine (*inset*); if the point is hot to the touch, the terrine is done.

Savoury Balls of Forcemeat

3 **Preparing meats.** Coarsely chop pork, veal, back fat, pig's liver and chicken livers. Chop an onion; stew it in butter until soft. Place the meats, the pre-cooked vegetables, two eggs, finely chopped garlic, chopped fresh parsley, dried basil and thyme, and ground spices—here, pepper, nutmeg, cloves and ginger—in a large bowl. Mix everything well by hand.

4 **Filling the terrine.** Line a terrine with thin sheets of pork back fat (*page 2*). If the sheets are long, let the ends hang over the sides. Fill the terrine with the prepared mixture. Mound the mixture slightly above the rim of the terrine (*above*)—it will shrink during cooking. To settle the contents, tap the terrine on a folded towel on the table.

1 **Forming meat balls.** Prepare a forcemeat with spinach and celery (*Steps 1 to 3, left*). Shape handfuls of the mixture into small balls. Cut caul (*page 3*) into pieces about 15 cm (6 inches) square; wrap each ball in a piece of caul (*above*). Pack the balls closely in a gratin dish; add enough water to cover the bottom of the dish.

6 **Weighting.** Place the terrine on a plate or tray. Leaving the foil in place, cover the top of the terrine with a wooden board that fits inside the rim. Distribute weights evenly on top of the board (*above*). Use scale weights, as here, or unopened cans.

7 **Serving the terrine.** Leave to cool for several hours. Remove the weights and the board, but not the foil; refrigerate the terrine overnight or preferably for three to four days. To serve, remove the foil and cut the terrine into slices about 1 cm (½ inch) thick. If you like, trim off the frame of white pork fat before serving.□

2 **Baking.** Set the dish, uncovered, in a 230°C (450°F or Mark 8) oven; bake for about 25 minutes. Place the dish under a hot grill for about 5 minutes to brown the meat balls. Serve them hot, or refrigerate them overnight to develop their flavour; serve cold.

Wine-Cooked Mussels in a Creamy Coating

A dry white wine blends especially well with shellfish, complementing its salty freshness. Only a relatively small amount of wine is required for steaming mussels, because they release liquid of their own while they cook. Herbs and aromatic vegetables, added to the pan, will bring extra flavour to the mussels—and fragrance to the liquid. A few minutes of steaming will open the bivalves and cook them.

Before cooking the mussels, they must be thoroughly cleaned (*Step 1*). Discard all mussels with broken shells, and those with shells that remain open when tapped smartly; such specimens are probably dead. Soak the live mussels in clean, salted water for about 30 minutes; they will expel any sand or grit they contain.

The cooking liquid can be served with the mussels just as it is, or it may be reduced by boiling to concentrate its flavours. Should the liquid taste very salty, however, do not reduce it, because the salt taste would increase; use any excess liquid, with water, in a stock or a soup.

If you like, you can enrich the liquid by adding a blend of egg yolks and cream (*right; recipe, page 37*). The addition of yolks and cream will also make the liquid less salty. Gentle heat will thicken the yolks slightly, giving extra body to the sauce. Alternatively, you can thicken the liquid with cubes of butter. Bring the liquid to the boil, turn the heat down to very low and put a fireproof mat under the pan. Whisk small cubes of butter into the liquid, a few at a time, making sure the butter does not turn oily.

1 Cleaning the mussels. Immerse fresh mussels in a bowl of cold salted water. Clean each mussel thoroughly; first pull off its hair-like beard, then scrape away any growth or debris from its shell, using a small sharp knife (*above*). Transfer the mussels to a fresh bowl of salted water. After soaking for about 30 minutes, the mussels will expel any sand or grit.

2 Adding wine. Strain the cleaned mussels and tip them all into a large pan. Add flavourings—here, celery sticks, garlic cloves, bay leaves, chopped parsley and thyme—and then pour in a generous splash of white wine (*above*). Cover the pan and set it over a high heat. Shaking the pan frequently, cook the mussels until their shells open—3 to 5 minutes.

5 Creating a sauce. Place egg yolks and double cream into a mixing bowl and whisk the ingredients to blend them. Pour in 2 to 3 ladlefuls of the cooking liquid (*above*), continuing to whisk until all the ingredients are smoothly amalgamated.

6 Adding the sauce. Pour the egg yolk and cream mixture over the mussels in the pan (*above*). As you are pouring, distribute the mixture so that each mussel is coated as evenly as possible with the liquid.

3 **Straining the mussels.** Pour the mussels into a colander lined with several layers of damp muslin, set over a deep bowl to catch the cooking liquid (*above*). Taste the liquid; if it is not salty, reduce it by boiling. If the liquid is too salty, use only part of it for the sauce; do not reduce it.

4 **Opening the shells.** When the mussels are cool enough to handle, prise the shells apart with your fingers and thumbs, separating the two halves completely (*above*). Discard the empty half shells. Arrange the mussels—still attached to the remaining half shells—in layers in a wide-surfaced shallow pan. Set the mussels aside.

7 **Finishing the dish.** Tilt the pan gently from side to side over a medium-low heat (*above*), until the sauce has thickened to a custard-like consistency—about 10 minutes; during this time, the sauce must never approach the boil, or it will curdle. Ladle the mussels into individual soup plates and serve immediately (*right*).□

Boiling Eggs for Shelling

Boiled, shelled eggs are useful garnishes as well as essential elements in many assembled dishes. The eggs may be soft-boiled or hard-boiled, depending on the use you intend to make of them.

The best eggs for shelling are three to four days old. The whites of new-laid eggs adhere firmly to the shell membrane, but after a few days they will have begun to shrink away from it, simplifying peeling.

Instead of plunging the eggs into boiling water, you can start them in cold water, which should be brought to a simmer over a medium heat (*Step 1, right*). Though it permits less precise timing, this method reduces the risk of the shells cracking through a sudden change of temperature at the beginning of cooking, while the relatively gentle heat makes for more tender whites. If you use this technique, time the eggs from the moment the water starts to bubble.

Eggs boiled for shelling run the gamut from the soft-yolked egg—the mollet egg of French cookery, used interchangeably with poached eggs in assembled dishes—to the hard-boiled egg, suitable for slicing and chopping, or for serving in a hot sauce as demonstrated on page 12. Do not overcook the eggs; boiling for more than 10 minutes from a cold-water start will produce a leathery, discoloured egg. This timing—and those given in the box on the right—are for size 2 eggs. Prepared similarly, extra large size 1 eggs will need slightly longer cooking, while smaller eggs will cook more rapidly. Deduct a minute from the times shown at each stage when using size 3 or 4 eggs, and up to 2 minutes for smaller sizes.

After boiling, the eggs should be plunged into cold water to arrest their cooking and to cool them for easy handling. Shelling, although not difficult, requires a light hand—particularly for soft mollet eggs, which are easily damaged. It is best to shell eggs just before use, as the shells protect the whites from drying out; but eggs can also be kept for a few hours out of their shells in a bowl of cold water, which will help keep the whites moist.

1 **Cooking the eggs.** Arrange the eggs loosely in a saucepan. Cover them generously with water, and place the pan over a medium heat (*above, left*). Time the eggs from the moment the bubbles begin to rise from the bottom of the pan (*above, right*). Adjust the heat to maintain a bare simmer. When the eggs have cooked for the time required, remove them from the pan and immediately plunge them into cold water to stop further cooking.

Gradations of Boiling

After 3 minutes. Started in cold water and cooked for 3 minutes from the moment the water comes to the boil, eggs have whites that have only partially set and yolks that are still liquid. These are the mollet eggs of French cooking. Allow 6 minutes to cook mollet eggs if they are started in boiling water.

After 4 minutes. The white is firmly set, as is most of the yolk, though the centre is still soft and dark yellow. This egg is easier to handle and to shell than the mollet egg; it can be used in the same way as a hard-boiled egg. To attain this consistency from a boiling-water start, the egg should be cooked for 8 minutes.

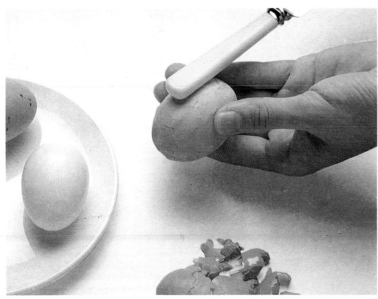

2 **Cracking the eggs.** Crack the shell of each egg by holding it gently in one hand and tapping it all over with the back of a spoon or the handle of a knife (*above*), taking care not to break the egg. The finely cracked shell will adhere to the inner membrane and can easily be peeled away from the surface of the white.

3 **Removing the shell.** Gently strip the shell away from the white of the egg, taking care to peel off the underlying membrane at the same time. Rinse off any remaining shell fragments by dipping the egg in water. If the peeled eggs are not required immediately, store them in a bowl of water to keep them from drying out.☐

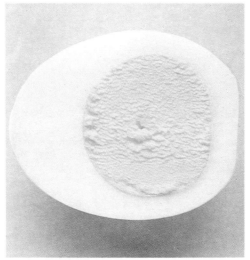

After 6 minutes. Both yolk and white are firmly set, although the centre of the yolk remains tender. This egg can be cut into quarters, sliced or chopped, but retains enough of its natural moisture to be briefly cooked as part of a further presentation. The equivalent timing for an egg started in boiling water is 10 minutes.

After 10 minutes. Yolk and white are both firmly set and the yolk is pale yellow in colour. This is the classic hard-boiled egg used for stuffing and as a garnish in cold dishes. Chopped or sliced, it can also be reheated in a sauce (*page 12*). Eggs require 12 minutes' cooking to hard-boil from a boiling-water start.

The effect of overcooking. If they are boiled for more than 10 minutes from a cold-water start—or 12 minutes if they are started in boiling water—egg whites turn rubbery and the yolks become dry and crumbly. Elements in the yolk and white interact to produce a green ring round the yolk—a sure sign of overcooking.

Sauced Egg Dishes

One of the most attractive ways of serving hard-boiled eggs is to cut them up and combine them with a hot sauce. In addition to reheating the eggs, the sauce also counterbalances their relative dryness. The dish may then be served without further embellishment, or else coated with breadcrumbs or grated cheese and given a rapid gratin finish.

Although the eggs should ideally be boiled immediately before use—since hard-boiled eggs lose some moisture in storage—leftover hard-boiled eggs will also give good results. If the eggs have been kept in the refrigerator, bring them to room temperature first to reduce the time they will need to warm through; otherwise the eggs may become rubbery through overcooking.

Any thick, well-flavoured sauce can be used to coat the eggs—including those made from vegetable purées, such as tomato sauce (*Basics booklet*) or the creamed sorrel sauce shown here (*recipe, page 37*). Sorrel lends a refreshing hint of tartness to the dish; for a milder effect, you could substitute creamed spinach (*recipe, page 38*). A gratin crust of crisp breadcrumbs adds another textural dimension. The crumbs will brown more evenly and have a finer flavour if they are first sautéed in butter (*Step 2, right, above*).

A thickened, flavoured white sauce also has sufficient body to complement hard-boiled eggs. In the lower demonstration (*recipe, page 38*), the sauce is prepared from a base of onions that have first been softened in butter. Like any roux-based sauce, the mixture needs lengthy simmering to rid it of the taste of raw flour. Near the end of cooking, egg yolks and herbs are stirred in for extra richness and flavour. The quartered eggs are added at the last minute; they need only be heated long enough to warm through.

There are many possible variations on this simple white sauce mixture. You can add extra ingredients—chopped chard leaves, for example—to the onions midway through cooking (*recipe, page 38*), or else enrich the finished sauce with double cream. To further extend the range of flavours, you could replace the milk in the sauce with a meat stock.

A Creamed Sorrel Gratin

1 Coating the eggs. Prepare a creamed sorrel purée (*recipe, page 37*). While the sorrel is stewing, boil eggs for about 10 minutes and then shell them (*page 11*). Cut the eggs in half lengthwise and place them in a buttered ovenproof dish, with their cut sides uppermost. Spoon the creamed sorrel over the eggs (*above*).

2 Preparing the breadcrumbs. Remove the crusts from pieces of stale bread; crumble the bread to make coarse breadcrumbs. Melt butter in a frying pan set over a low heat. Stirring continuously, cook the breadcrumbs for about 5 to 6 minutes, until they turn a golden-brown.

A Complement of Milk-Stewed Onions

1 Starting the onions. Melt butter in a heavy pan set over a low heat. Cut the onions crosswise into thick slices and add them to the butter (*above*). Stir until the onions are well coated with butter. If you like, season with salt and pepper.

2 Incorporating flour. Cover the pan, and set it over a fireproof mat and allow the onions to cook at a gentle simmer. After 8 to 10 minutes, when the onions have softened and become a pale golden colour, sprinkle flour over them. Stir the onions thoroughly, until the flour and the butter form a smooth paste.

3 **Assembling the gratin.** Remove the breadcrumbs from the heat. After about 1 minute, when the crumbs are cool enough to handle, use your fingers to sprinkle them liberally over the surface of the sorrel-coated eggs (*above*).

4 **Serving the eggs.** Place the dish in a preheated, 200°C (400°F or Mark 6) oven. Cook for about 15 minutes, until the mixture is heated through and the surface is lightly browned. Remove the dish from the oven and serve the eggs on to warmed plates, including some of the gratin topping in each portion. □

3 **Making the sauce.** Pour milk on to the onion mixture (*above*). Turn up the heat and stir continuously while the sauce comes to the boil. Reduce the heat and leave the sauce to simmer for 25 to 30 minutes to cook the flour thoroughly.

4 **Adding the eggs.** While the sauce is simmering, hard boil and shell some eggs. Chop the eggs into quarters. Stir two or three raw egg yolks into the sauce to enrich it; for extra piquancy, you can sprinkle on some herbs—in this case, chopped parsley. Add the quartered hard-boiled eggs to the sauce (*above*).

5 **Serving the sauced eggs.** Leave the pan over the heat for 2 to 3 minutes to warm the eggs through. Serve the eggs directly on individual warmed plates. Or you could transfer the eggs to a shallow, buttered ovenproof dish and give them a rapid gratin finish in the oven or under a hot grill (*Steps 2 to 4, above*). □

Game Birds that Benefit from Special Treatment

To be enjoyed at their best, roasted grouse and wild duck must be treated differently from other game birds. The legs of both birds should be removed after roasting—as demonstrated here—but in each case this step is taken for a different reason.

The legs of grouse (*right*) have bitter flesh, so when the bird is roasted, only the delicately flavoured breast is served (*recipe, page 39*). The roasted legs are best kept for stocks or pies, where prolonged cooking will moderate their bitterness.

Wild duck's legs are set further underneath the body than are the legs of other game birds, so at the point when the breast is roasted to perfection, the heat will not have penetrated sufficiently to cook the legs. The solution to this discrepancy is to serve the breast as a separate course, while finishing the legs under the grill. Here, the breasts are served on toast that has been spread with a *farce gratin* (*recipe, page 39*) made of duck and chicken livers. The grilled legs, presented after this rich dish, are best partnered by a light garnish, such as a fresh salad.

Bringing Out the Best in Grouse

1 **Roasting the game birds.** Truss the grouse (*Basics booklet*); and bard them by tying on sheets of pork back fat. Season them with salt and pepper. Put them in a fireproof dish or roasting pan and roast them in an oven preheated to 230°C (450°F or Mark 8) for about 15 minutes. To brown the breasts, remove the birds from the oven, cut the barding strings (*above*) and remove and discard the bards. Return the birds to the oven for a further 5 minutes, until their breasts are lightly browned.

Wild Duck in Two Courses

1 **Roasting the birds.** Truss and bard wild ducks—here, mallards—(*Step 1, above*), and season them. Put them in a fireproof dish and roast them in an oven preheated to 200°C (400°F or Mark 6). After about 15 minutes, remove the birds; discard the bards. Return the birds to the oven for 5 minutes to brown the breasts.

2 **Carving the birds.** Discard the trussing strings from the birds. To carve each bird, set it on a wooden board, hold it steady with the rounded side of a carving fork and use a slender, flexible knife to cut through the flesh between the breast and the leg to expose the joint; slice down through the joint to remove the leg (*above, left*). Repeat to remove the other leg; set aside the legs. To carve the breast, use the knife to cut it cleanly into large slices (*above, right*).

2 **Removing the legs.** Cut through the trussing string and pull it free. To prepare each bird for serving, partially carve it to remove the legs. Steady the breast of the grouse with a carving fork and use a knife with a flexible blade to cut through the bird below the breast section, cutting away the legs (*above*).

3 **Garnishing the birds.** Place the trimmed birds on a serving platter with a garnish of fresh watercress. Prepare bread sauce (*recipe, page 39*). If you like, you can prepare a contrasting bread garnish— here, pieces of crustless bread are sautéed in butter and served with the birds (*above*).

4 **Serving the grouse.** As a single serving, present each diner with a whole grouse breast and some of the crisp, sautéed bread pieces. Hand the bread sauce round separately in a sauceboat.□

3 **Serving the breast.** Trim the crusts from a loaf of bread. Cut the bread into slices similar in size to the breast slices; toast the bread. Spread the toast with a *farce gratin* (*recipe, page 39*). Serve each person with some toast, slices of the breast (*above*) and a few drops of the juices that were released during carving.

4 **Serving the legs.** To finish cooking the legs, place them on a preheated grill. Keeping the heat high, grill the legs for 7 to 8 minutes, then turn them over and grill the other sides for the same amount of time. Serve the duck legs as soon as they are done—accompanied, if you like, by a salad (*above*).□

Sweet-and-Sour Spareribs

A Barbecue Baked in the Oven

Spareribs—a thin cut from pork belly—lend themselves equally well to grilling or roasting. The ribs can be basted liberally with a highly seasoned sauce as they cook—both to flavour the meat and to create a rich surface glaze.

Like most fresh pork cuts, spareribs will have more flavour if they are salted down overnight with herbs (*recipe, page 42*); they should be wiped dry before cooking, though some herbs can be left on to add extra flavour. They can then be set in a hot oven for 10 minutes to draw off fat. Although the ribs can be separated for cooking, they will retain their juices and be easier to handle if kept in rack form.

Piquant sauces that combine strongly flavoured ingredients are traditional accompaniments to spareribs in Oriental and Western cuisines. A barbecue sauce that has been simmered to reduce and thicken it can be coated on to the meat as it cooks (*Step 6, below; recipe, page 40*). Thinner mixtures can be used first to marinate the ribs, and then to baste during cooking (*opposite page, below; or recipe, page 40*).

1 Starting the sauce. Place all the solid ingredients—here, a seeded and chopped chili pepper, a crushed garlic clove, mustard powder and mixed herbs—in a mortar. Pound them to a smooth paste using a pestle. Then add the liquid ingredients—in this case, the juice of half an orange and equal amounts of vinegar and honey.

2 Sieving the mixture. Stir the ingredients together, then pour the mixture into a bowl through a sieve, to separate out the pieces of chili pepper; these are discarded. Use the pestle to press the other ingredients through the sieve.

6 Coating with the sauce. Remove the pan from the oven. Tip the pan and spoon off any fat that has exuded. With a ladle pour just enough sauce over the ribs to coat them thickly (*above*). Lower the oven temperature to 180°C (350°F or Mark 4), and return the pan to the oven.

7 Cooking the ribs. Baste the meat at 10 minute intervals with the sauce and pan juices. If the pan dries out, add extra sauce or a little water. When the sauce has formed a thick glaze on the ribs—this takes about 45 minutes—remove the pan from the oven.

8 Carving and serving the ribs. Holding the meat steady with a fork, divide each rack into serving portions by slicing with a sharp, heavy knife between the ribs. Place the carved portions on a serving plate; here, they are garnished with sprigs of watercress.□

3 **Cooking onions and tomatoes.** Chop an onion finely and stew it gently in a little oil until soft. Add peeled, chopped and seeded fresh tomatoes; alternatively, use canned tomatoes strained through a sieve (*above*). Raise the heat slightly.

4 **Mixing and heating the sauce.** Pour the other sieved sauce ingredients into the pan and blend them with the onion and tomatoes. Bring the sauce to the boil, stirring constantly. Lower the heat until the sauce is barely simmering, then leave it for about 30 minutes to reduce by half, stirring it from time to time.

5 **Drawing fat from the spareribs.** If the spareribs have been salted down, dry them with a cloth or paper towels. Rub off loose herbs and salt, leaving a sparse coating on the ribs. Place the ribs in an ungreased roasting pan and roast at a high heat—200°C (400°F or Mark 6)— for 10 minutes to draw out fat.

A Tangy Marinade for Cooking over Coals

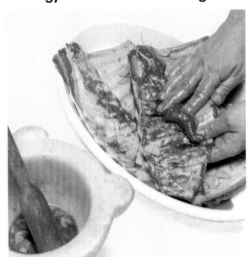

1 **Marinating the spareribs.** In a mortar, pound garlic and assorted spices— here, cloves, cinnamon and allspice— to a paste. Mix in slices of peeled ginger root and the liquid ingredients of the marinade—in this case, soy sauce, honey and sherry. Rub the mixture into the meat (*above*). Marinate the ribs for up to 4 hours, turning them 2 or 3 times.

2 **Grilling the ribs.** Remove the ribs from the marinade. Strain the marinade to remove the ginger slices. Place the ribs on a grill rack and set them to grill at a medium heat. Brown both sides, then baste the top with the marinade— applied here with rosemary branches. When the basted side has dried, turn the ribs and baste the other side.

3 **Carving the racks.** Turn the ribs several times, basting repeatedly. After about 30 minutes, when both sides have glazed crisply, transfer the ribs to a serving dish or carving board. Holding the meat steady with the back of a carving fork (*above*), cut between ribs to divide the rack into serving portions.□

How to Chop Raw Meat by Hand—and Why

When a meat dish is not supported by sauces, strong seasonings or long cooking, it is particularly important that the basic ingredients should be perfect. If the key ingredient is minced beef or veal, the cook who chops it by hand can make doubly sure that the meat is immaculately fresh and free of unwanted fat and gristle.

Steak tartare—a dish of raw, chopped steak—is an appropriate case in point. For this dish to have flawless colour and texture, the meat should be trimmed of fat and chopped as close to eating time as practicable—ideally, within minutes. Chopped steak at the pinnacle of freshness needs seasonings only to flatter the flavour, never to disguise it.

While hand-chopped meat is virtually a requirement for steak tartare, its special texture (*box, opposite*) will also improve any lightly cooked dish: sautéed veal *fricadelles* (*recipe, page 41*), for example. Hamburgers are unusually delicious to eat when made with hand-chopped beef and cooked—preferably rare—with the same respect that you would give a prime steak. (For meat loaves and braised or poached meat balls, which cook for a longer time, the advantages of hand chopping are not so conspicuous, and butcher's mince is quite satisfactory.)

The best equipment for chopping meat is a pair of heavy cook's knives that are the same length and of equal weight. With matched knives, you can easily achieve a chopping rhythm that will permit the heft of the cutlery to do most of the work. If you lack two such knives, don't try to improvise; a single knife will do the job better than two that are out of balance. But whether you use two knives or one, be sure the blade has a keen edge; a dull edge will mash the meat into an unpleasant pulp instead of cutting it cleanly.

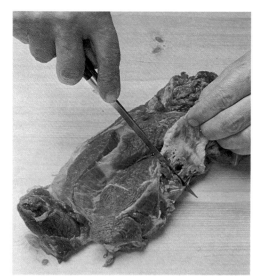

1 **Trimming the meat.** Using a very sharp knife, cut the meat away from the bone, if any, then divide it along the muscle seams into lean sections, paring away all sinewy connective tissue. The cut being trimmed here is chuck—a good choice for hamburgers or steak tartare, since its flavour is excellent and the mincing makes it certain to be perfectly tender.

2 **Cubing.** Trim off every trace of fat and membrane from the meat, and cut the trimmed sections of lean meat coarsely into fairly small cubes. The mincing will proceed more swiftly if you start with the meat in pieces of roughly uniform size.

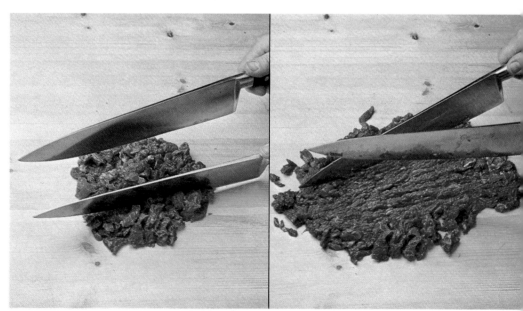

3 **Mincing.** Spread the cubed meat in a single layer and chop it with a matched pair of heavy, sharp knives, moving them alternately and rhythmically, as if beating a drum. Work with a loose-wristed action, holding the knives more or less parallel to each other in a relaxed grip and letting their weight do most of the work for you. As the chopping progresses the meat pieces will

A Butcher's Mince Versus Your Own

Meat ground up by the butcher and sold as minced beef (*far right*) is usually thoroughly laced with fat. Beef trimmed and chopped by hand (*near right*) is not only leaner, it has a noticeably different texture from the machine-minced beef. Mechanical mincers mash and mangle the fibres and, in the process, juices are lost. With hand-chopped meat the fibres are cut rather than crushed, and so retain more of their moisture. The particles of the meat, whether finely or coarsely chopped, stay separate even during subsequent mixing and cooking, giving the finished dish a distinctive texture.

Cooks who have electric food processors may want to try mincing meat with them. The machines can produce a perfectly smooth meat purée that suits many Mediterranean meat ball recipes—Greek *keftedes tiganites* for example (*recipe, page 42*). But food processors are unsuitable when a coarser mince is needed, as for hamburgers.

begin to spread out; stop from time to time and use one of the knife blades to flip the edges of the chopped mass back into the centre, turning the mass over each time. This helps to achieve a consistent texture. Continue chopping until the meat is minced as coarsely or finely as your preference or the recipe dictates.□

The Basic Hamburger and Ways to Vary It

According to one of many accounts of its origin, the ubiquitous hamburger began as a dish of raw, chopped beef eaten by the inhabitants of Baltic Russia and was introduced in cooked form to Hamburg by German traders; then, some time in the 19th century, it is supposed to have been brought to the United States by German immigrants. By the simple expedient of serving the meat in a soft bun the Americans produced a substantial snack that could be eaten conveniently in the hand. In this guise, the minced beef patty is familiar throughout the world.

Although the hamburger has suffered rough treatment at the hands of snack-bar cooks, at its best—made from good quality beef, cooked rare, with a juicy red heart—it stands comparison with steak. Like a steak, the hamburger can be either grilled or fried. Grilling—especially over charcoal or wood embers—adds flavour, but the meat needs skilful treatment so that it does not dry up: the cut edges of the mince can exude a lot of moisture unless the hamburger is effectively seared. In pan frying, any juices that the hamburger yields stay in the pan and can be recaptured by deglazing: pouring a little wine or water into the pan and stirring to dissolve the meat residues.

A lean cut of beef, such as rump, makes ideal mince for hamburgers. Less expensive cuts—topside or chuck, for example, or even neck or flank if carefully trimmed of all connective tissue—are also excellent; they have a good flavour and, when minced, cannot be tough. For a really juicy hamburger, with a coarse or fine texture as you prefer, chop the meat by hand, as explained on the previous pages.

Many people like the flavour and moistness imparted to hamburgers by the inclusion of a certain proportion of fat with the meat. But undercooked beef fat is not easily digested, so if you like rare hamburgers, use lean meat and mix it with a little butter or—even better—raw beef marrow. Season the meat mixture before cooking, but use a light hand: your aim is to bring out the flavour of the meat, not to conceal it.

When you shape the patties, handle the mixture gently; a loosely formed hamburger cooks more evenly and has a more appetizing texture than a compact patty but it must be firm enough to hold together while it cooks. Fry the hamburger just as you would a steak. Turn it once, using a spatula to prevent it from crumbling. Hamburgers can be served with a wide variety of sauces or garnishes, and even patties simply destined for the traditional bun may profit from a sauce made with the deglazed pan juices.

1 **Seasoning the beef.** Using your fingers, lightly toss the minced meat together with whatever seasonings you are using. Chopped fresh dill is shown above, but you can substitute any other fresh or dried herb that you like, or grated cheese, fried onion, or minced capers.

2 **Shaping the patties.** Divide the mixture into portions and form each one into a ball. Flatten the ball on the top and bottom to give a good surface for searing but do not squash the patty. For a rare hamburger, make the patty as thick as 4 cm (2 inches); for well-cooked hamburgers, scale down the thickness to 2 cm (1 inch) so that the outside does not dry up before the middle is done.

3 **Searing the hamburgers.** Heat a film of oil in a frying pan set over high heat. When the oil is hot, add the patties and fry them for 3 to 5 minutes. Turn them over and sear the second side. Lower the heat, and finish cooking them to your taste.

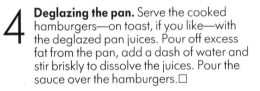

4 **Deglazing the pan.** Serve the cooked hamburgers—on toast, if you like—with the deglazed pan juices. Pour off excess fat from the pan, add a dash of water and stir briskly to dissolve the juices. Pour the sauce over the hamburgers.□

Adding a Surprise Stuffing

One way to vary the nature of hamburgers is by mixing the raw chopped steak with any number of additions (*Step 1, opposite page*). But another way to lend variety is to conceal a stuffing of contrasting character and flavour in the heart of a hamburger (*right*).

A nugget of soft cheese is a good basis for a hamburger stuffing. The Roquefort cheese shown here has a sharp enough flavour of its own, but you might prefer a mild curd or cottage cheese, accented with capers or chopped anchovies or olives. The possibilities for improvisation are almost limitless. Try enclosing a pocket of chopped cooked vegetables, such as mushrooms or carrots, in the hamburger. Or, for a crunchy stuffing, you could add a mixture of chopped nuts with chopped parsley and onions.

1 **Filling the patties.** To stuff a hamburger, simply press a cavity in the middle of it with your thumb, add the filling and close the meat around it. Shape the patty carefully and cook it in the usual way.

2 **Finishing touches.** In this hamburger, the Roquefort cheese centre comes as a creamy surprise to the diner. You could use a harder cheese like cheddar for a different flavour, or chopped chives or spring onions mashed into a soft cheese.

Savoury Fillings for Hollowed-Out Fruits

Many fruits with a central stone, core or mass of seeds are easily hollowed out to provide containers for savoury fillings. Baked until the fruit casing is tender, these simple assemblies may be served as a main dish or as an accompaniment.

The choice of filling ingredients for fruits is a very wide one. Minced raw beef or lamb, roasted or boiled chicken, or sautéed chicken livers are all good foundations. Or you could base the filling on nuts, aromatic vegetables such as onion, or dried fruit. Aromatic fruits such as quince would suit a mild-flavoured stuffing; sweet fruits, such as papayas, go well with spicy mixtures. The only rule is that all ingredients should be finely chopped to give the filling an even consistency.

In the dish demonstrated on the right (*recipe, page 43*)—a Caribbean speciality—papayas, halved and seeded, are filled with a spicy beef mixture, then sprinkled with grated cheese, baked, and served with a tomato sauce. Apples, pears and quinces, cored and stuffed with lamb

and aromatics, are a feature of Middle-Eastern cookery. And apples filled with sage and onions (*below*) are a traditional English accompaniment to be served with grilled or roasted pork.

The preparation of fruit for stuffing will depend on the type of fruit used. Papayas become very soft when fully ripe. Since fruits to be stuffed should be firm enough to hold their shape, these are best used slightly underripe, peeled and parboiled to soften them somewhat before they are filled and baked. Firm-fleshed fruits do not require parboiling. Apples and pears may be baked peeled or unpeeled, but quinces should always be peeled, as their skins are tough and bitter.

Whatever the fruit, bake it in a well-buttered ovenproof dish, and baste the fruit frequently with butter and cooking juices to prevent it drying out. In the case of firm-fleshed fruit, a little water in the baking dish will keep the fruit moist as it bakes, and ensure that it does not stick to the baking sheet or burn.

Stuffed Papaya Shells

1 **Preparing fruit.** Peel underripe papayas, cut them in half lengthwise and scoop out the seeds with a spoon. Plunge the papaya halves into boiling, salted water and parboil them for 10 minutes to soften them; the flesh will deepen in colour during this process. Lift out the papayas (*above*), drain them, and pat them dry with kitchen paper.

Apples Packed with Sage and Onions

1 **Coring apples.** Wrap a large onion in foil and bake in a preheated 180°C (350°F or Mark 4) oven for about 1 hour, until soft. Meanwhile, peel firm, crisp apples—here, russet apples are used—and core them. Using a small knife, cut round each central cavity to enlarge it (*above*). Place each peeled apple in acidulated water to stop it discolouring.

2 **Filling the fruit.** Peel and finely chop the baked onion. Chop one fresh sage leaf for each apple, then mix the chopped sage and onion together. Season the mixture. Butter a shallow baking dish and add a little water. Place the apples in the dish and spoon the onion mixture into the cavities. Dot each apple with butter.

3 **Baking and serving.** Bake the stuffed apples in a preheated 180°C (350°F or Mark 4) oven for 45 minutes to 1 hour, until the fruit is tender. Serve the apples hot to accompany roast pork or, as here, grilled pork chops.□

2 **Making the stuffing.** Peel and chop tomatoes. Seed and chop a red or green chili pepper. Sauté chopped onion and garlic and minced lean beef in oil for 15 minutes, stirring to prevent the meat burning. Add the chopped tomatoes and chili pepper and season; blend the ingredients (*above*) and cook for a few minutes until the mixture thickens.

3 **Filling the fruits.** Generously butter a shallow baking dish. Spoon the meat mixture into the papaya halves so as to fill the cavity in each one and form a small mound over the top (*above*). Place the filled halves in the baking dish.

4 **Adding cheese.** For a crisp gratin finish, sprinkle the filled halves with grated hard cheese such as Gruyère or the Parmesan used here. To prevent the fruit from drying out or browning while in the oven dot the surface of each papaya half with butter.

5 **Baking and serving.** Bake the stuffed fruit in a preheated 180°C (350°F or Mark 4) oven for about 30 minutes, until the fruit is tender and the cheese has melted and browned slightly. Serve the stuffed fruit hot, accompanied by melted butter or, as here, a tomato sauce.☐

A Moulded Custard with a Caramel Glaze

To make a successful moulded custard that sets firmly enough to be turned out, the proportion of egg white to yolk is critical. Too much white will produce a coarse, rubbery-textured custard; too little will produce a custard that will collapse when it is unmoulded. A ratio of four whole eggs and four egg yolks to every 60 cl (1 pint) of liquid provides the correct balance.

Such custards can be flavoured with finely grated orange or lemon peel, chocolate, coffee or vanilla, and baked in an oiled mould; but the classic version of the dessert is the *crème caramel* demonstrated here (*recipe, page 44*). *Crème caramel* is a vanilla custard which has been baked in a caramelized mould (*box, below*). As the custard cooks, the hard caramel lining melts in the heat, allowing the cooked custard to slide easily out of the mould. When the custard is turned out, it is capped with a layer of caramel and surrounded by a caramel sauce.

1 Adding custard to a mould. In a bowl, beat together the whole eggs, egg yolks, sugar, a few drops of vanilla extract and a pinch of salt. Stirring continuously, pour hot milk on to the mixture. Strain, then skim off any foam from the surface. Place a caramelized mould (*box, below*) in an ovenproof dish and ladle the mixture into the mould (*above*).

2 Testing for doneness. Pour warm water into the dish to immerse the mould to two-thirds of its depth. Bake the custard for 1 hour in a warm oven, preheated to 170°C (325°F or Mark 3). Test that the custard has set by inserting a knife into it. The knife should come out clean: if it does not (*above*), cook the custard for a further 10 minutes, then test again.

Caramelizing a Mould

1 Making the caramel. In a heavy pan over a low heat, dissolve sugar in a little water. Cook over moderate heat until the mixture is a light amber colour (*above*). Stop the cooking by dipping the pan momentarily in a bowl of ice-cubes and water.

2 Coating the mould. Immediately, pour the caramel into a warmed, dry mould. Using oven gloves, pick up the mould and rotate it so that the caramel runs round the inside of the mould, coating it completely. Allow the excess caramel to form a layer on the base.

3 Oiling the mould. To prevent the custard from sticking to the mould, use a pastry brush to put a little almond oil—or tasteless vegetable oil—on any areas of the mould that remain uncoated with caramel (*above*).

3 **Loosening the custard.** Remove the mould from the oven dish and leave it to cool. When the custard is tepid, insert a knife a little way down the side of the mould and run it round (*above*) to free the sides of the custard.

4 **Freeing the custard.** Hold the mould steady with one hand and use the fingertips of the other hand to ease the custard from the sides of the mould by pressing gently on the surface (*above*). Continue until the custard is not sticking to the mould at any point.

5 **Unmoulding the custard.** Choose a serving plate deep enough to hold the liquid caramel that will run down the sides of the custard as you unmould it. Invert the plate on to the custard and turn both over together. Lift the mould gently from the custard (*above*). Serve the *crème caramel* tepid, or chill it for a few hours in the refrigerator.□

Methods of Preparing Nuts

Nuts are an indispensable ally in sweet cookery. They can be used to decorate anything from a petit four to a dumpling. Chopped, grated or finely ground, they add flavour and texture to fillings, cake batters, meringues and pastry doughs. Nuts can also be combined with sugar to make marzipan (*opposite page, centre; recipe, page 45*)—or to make praline, a brittle confection (*boxes, below; recipes, page 45*) that adds a crunchy texture to buttercreams and meringues.

After shelling, nuts are usually peeled to rid them of their bitter inner coat. Almonds and pistachio nuts are easier to peel if they are parboiled first (*right, above*). Most other nuts respond to dry roasting, after which their skins can be rubbed off (*opposite page, above, left*). The tight, inner skin of coconut can be peeled off with a knife (*right*).

Nuts should be chopped with a heavy knife (*opposite page, above, middle*), or ground in a food processor (*opposite page, above, right*). Ground nuts—usually almonds—are mixed with icing sugar and bound with egg white to form marzipan. Kneaded into a small ball, the mixture can be rolled out and cut into decorative shapes or used as a cake filling or topping.

Whole or finely ground nuts can be combined with sugar and caramelized to make praline, or mixed with sugar syrup to make white praline. Both mixtures are cooled, then crushed to a powder.

Blanching to Loosen Skins

1 **Loosening the skins.** Tip shelled nuts—here, almonds are used—into a pan of boiling water (*above*); parboil them for about a minute. Drain the nuts.

2 **Rubbing off the skins.** Spread out a towel and tip the parboiled nuts on to it; fold the towel over them (*above*). Rub the nuts vigorously in the folded towel until they have all shed their skins.

Opening and Grating a Coconut

1 **Cracking the coconut.** Remove the tuft to expose the eyes; pierce them with a skewer and drain the liquid. Use the back of a cleaver to crack the seam near the nut's base; it will open along the seam.

2 **Grating the flesh.** Use a knife to divide the flesh inside the nut into sections. Insert the knife behind each section to prise it loose from the shell. Cut away the brown outer skin. Finely grate the flesh (*above*).

Praline: a Brittle Amalgam of Nuts and Caramel

1 **Caramelizing the nuts.** Put blanched almonds and sugar into a heavy pan. Using a wooden spoon, stir over a low heat until the sugar melts and turns a pale amber. Remove from the heat.

2 **Cooling the mixture.** Pour the mixture on to an oiled marble slab or baking sheet. While still hot, quickly spread it out with the spoon; leave to cool and harden.

3 **Crushing the praline.** Break the cooled praline into pieces and put in a strong plastic bag. Holding the bag closed with one hand, use a rolling pin to crush the praline until it forms coarse crumbs.

Parching Off Papery Skins

Peeling roasted nuts. Tip nuts—here, hazelnuts—on to a baking sheet; roast in a preheated 170°C (325°F or Mark 3) oven for about 10 minutes. Transfer the nuts to a towel; rub off the skins.

A Neat Method of Chopping

Pivoting a knife. Using a heavy knife, coarsely chop nuts—here, pecan nuts. Press on the tip with one hand and pivot the blade in an arc while moving it up and down to chop the nuts more finely.

Pulverizing in a Processor

Grinding the nuts. Put peeled nuts—here, almonds—into a food processor. Grind in short bursts, using a spatula to push down nuts that cling to the sides, until a coarse-textured flour results.

A Firm Paste from Ground Almonds

1 **Mixing nuts and sugar.** Squeeze lemon juice and lightly beat egg whites. Blanch almonds, grind them in a processor and place them in a bowl. Stir sifted icing sugar into the ground nuts (*above*).

2 **Adding egg white.** To prevent sticking, use a knife to stir the lemon juice and a little egg white into the almond mixture. Add more egg, a little at a time, mixing it in by hand to make a stiff paste.

3 **Kneading the paste.** Lightly sprinkle a work surface—here, marble—with icing sugar. Gather the paste into a ball and knead it lightly—do not overwork the paste or it will become oily.

4 **Sieving the praline.** Put the praline in a coarse-meshed metal sieve set over a bowl. Use your fingertips to force the praline through the sieve. Return large pieces to the bag and crush them again.

White Praline: a Soft Variation

1 **Adding nuts.** Cook a sugar syrup to the hard-ball stage (*Basics booklet*). Off the heat, add finely ground almonds and stir them in. Pour the mixture on to an oiled marble slab, spread it out to cool.

2 **Sieving the white praline.** Break the cooled praline into pieces with your hands. Using a wooden spoon, press the praline through a metal sieve (*above*).

Transforming Meringue with Nuts

When ground nuts are added to a basic meringue mixture they contribute more than flavour: the nuts transform the texture of the finished product. After baking, nut meringues—often known by their French name *japonais*—are crisp and firm on the outside with a distinctive, chewy interior (*recipe, page 46*).

The best nuts for mixing into the uncooked meringue are those with a delicate flavour. Almonds and hazelnuts are the most common choices; if you like, you can combine the two. Once mixed, the meringue should be piped out quickly; oil from the nuts will soon cause the foam of egg whites and sugar to subside.

Since *japonais* is denser than other meringues, it is piped in thin, flat shapes which cook through evenly. When they are baked, the flat shapes—usually discs or ovals—lend themselves well to being stacked two or three deep and interspersed with layers of filling.

Nut-flavoured fillings complement *japonais* perfectly. You can use whipped cream—plain or liqueur-flavoured—and stir in ground or chopped nuts. Walnuts, hazelnuts, pistachio nuts or blanched almonds are all suitable. Nuts in any form also blend well with buttercream (*recipe, page 46*). For a particularly light effect use the meringue buttercream in this demonstration—here, mixed with praline.

When the layers have been stacked, the assembly can be decorated with a topping of chocolate frosting (*recipe, page 45*) or fondant icing (*Basics booklet*). A traditional finish for nut-flavoured meringues is a coating of chopped nuts or praline, pressed into a layer of buttercream. The buttercream will be easier to apply to the top and sides of the meringues if the assemblies are chilled first. Praline gives the cakes a crunchy amber-coloured exterior; for a softer coating, use white praline (*box, right*). Finally, use a knife to press decorative ridges into the soft surfaces of the cakes, as shown right, or add a simple garnish such as chocolate frills (*Step 5, opposite*). To make the frills, pour melted chocolate on to a baking sheet, spread it evenly and let it set. Push a metal spatula at an angle along the surface of the hardened chocolate—the thin layer of chocolate will curl up into a frill.

1 **Adding almonds.** Line a baking sheet with silicon paper and draw oval guidelines with a pencil. Grind almonds (*page 27*) and sieve them into a small bowl; mix in castor sugar. In a large bowl, beat egg whites until they form soft peaks. Add sugar, a little at a time, and whisk until the peaks are stiff. Fold in the almond mixture (*above*).

2 **Piping the meringue.** Insert a plain 5 mm ($\frac{1}{4}$ inch) nozzle into a piping bag and fill it two-thirds full with meringue. Working from the outside of each oval inwards, pipe spirals of meringue (*above*). Bake the ovals in a 170°C (325°F or Mark 3) oven until they turn a pale gold—about 50 minutes—then cool them.

A Fluffy Effect from White Praline

1 **Making round cakes.** Pipe *japonais*— here, into 5 cm (2 inch) rounds. Bake them (*Steps 1 and 2, above*). Sandwich them in pairs with meringue buttercream (*recipe, page 46*). Refrigerate the meringues, then coat them with buttercream. Prepare white praline (*page 27*); press it on to the surfaces. Press three lines into the tops.

2 **Serving the meringues.** When you have decorated all the meringues, transfer them to a serving plate lined with a napkin. Arrange the finished meringues in a single layer so that their patterned upper surfaces are clearly displayed.

3 **Preparing a filling.** In a large bowl, make buttercream—here, made with Italian meringue (*recipe, page 46*). Prepare praline, crushed and sieved until fine (*page 26*). Reserve two-thirds of the praline, and add the rest to the bowl of buttercream (*above*). Using a wooden spoon, beat the two together.

4 **Assembling the cakes.** Free the meringues from the paper; if they have spread unevenly during baking, trim the edges with a small, sharp knife. Using a metal spatula, spread the upper surface of a meringue with the buttercream, then press another meringue gently on top; place the sandwiched meringues on a tray. Refrigerate them for about 20 minutes to firm the filling. Hold each assembly in your hand and spread first the sides and then the top with the buttercream (*above, left*). Hold the cake over the reserved praline and gently press it on to the surfaces (*above, right*).

5 **Finishing the meringues.** If you like, you can decorate the meringues with small chocolate shapes, such as the frills used here. Since chocolate frills are fragile, use a small spatula or a knife to transfer them to the cakes (*above*). Use a cake slice to serve the meringues (*right*). □

Decorative Patisserie from a Creamed Batter

Individual moulds will shape a batter as it bakes, producing little cakes of perfect symmetry. Fluted moulds—circles, ovals or diamonds—yield shapes which are decorative in themselves. You can place a simple garnish, such as chopped nuts, on the cakes before they are baked (*right*) or you can ice them afterwards. Plain deep tins, such as dariole moulds, produce cakes with smooth surfaces for more elaborate coatings—here, raspberry jam and freshly grated coconut (*right, below*).

An ideal batter for these little cakes includes generous amounts of butter and eggs, so that the texture will be moist and tender. To make such a batter (*recipe, page 46*), butter is beaten on its own and then beaten a second time with sugar. This forces air into the butter, which lightens the mixture. To achieve a homogeneous blend, eggs are added one at a time. Finally, flour is folded in, with baking powder, which helps to raise the batter.

For a selection of cakes, you can divide the batter into batches and add a different flavouring to each. Cocoa, sifted with the flour, will add colour and flavour, or you can stir chopped nuts, dried fruit or crystallized peel into the finished batter.

To ensure that the batter does not stick, cake moulds should be carefully prepared each time you use them. Each mould must be thoroughly buttered, then coated with flour. Alternatively, you can stand paper cases—which do not require buttering or flouring—inside bun tins. The cases are removed when the cakes are eaten. You can spoon batter into small moulds or cases, but a piping bag is the best way of filling deep, narrow tins. The batter will expand during baking, so the moulds or cases should be only two-thirds full.

When the baked cakes have been unmoulded and allowed to cool, they are ready for the decoration of your choice. Choose an icing or buttercream (*recipe, page 46*) topping to match or contrast with the flavour of the batter. Another method of decorating moulded cakes—especially those baked in shallow round tins—is to slice the tops off the cakes and pipe on fresh cream or buttercream. The cake tops, cut in half, are set into the cream to resemble butterfly wings (*recipe, page 47*).

Decorative Moulds for a Simple Finish

1 Adding eggs. Put soft butter in a mixing bowl and beat with a wooden spoon until the butter is pale. Add sugar and beat until the mixture is light and fluffy. Break an egg into the mixture and beat it well (*above*). Add the rest of the eggs, one by one, beating well after each addition.

2 Adding flour. Sift together flour and baking powder—for maximum aeration, sift the flour mixture several times. With a metal spoon, fold a little of the flour mixture into the creamed batter (*above*). Fold in the remaining flour mixture a little at a time to combine it evenly.

Miniature Towers with a Coconut Coating

1 Filling moulds. Coat the inside of dariole moulds with butter; sprinkle them with flour. Set the moulds on a baking sheet. Prepare a creamed batter (*Steps 1 and 2, above*); spoon the batter into a piping bag fitted with a plain, medium-sized nozzle. Fill the moulds two-thirds full. Tap the moulds to settle the mixture.

2 Trimming the cakes. Bake the cakes in a preheated 190°C (375°F or Mark 5) oven for 15 minutes, or until golden-brown. When they are cool enough to handle, unmould on to a wire rack. Let them cool completely, then place one in a clean mould. Using the rim of the mould as a guide, slice off the top of the cake.

3 **Filling moulds.** Brush the inside of little fluted moulds with softened butter using a pastry brush. Sprinkle flour over the butter and tip out the excess flour. Place the moulds on a baking sheet. Take a teaspoonful of batter and, with another spoon, push the batter into a mould until it is two-thirds full (*above*). Fill the rest of the moulds in the same way.

4 **Adding nuts.** Tap each mould lightly on the baking sheet to settle the batter. To create a crunchy surface, sprinkle sugar over the batter. Place a few chopped nuts—here, flaked almonds—on the top of each cake (*above*).

5 **Unmoulding the cakes.** Bake the cakes in a preheated 190°C (375°F or Mark 5) oven for 15 minutes, or until they are golden-brown. Remove them from the oven and leave them until they are cool enough to handle—about 10 minutes. Unmould the cakes on to your hand (*above*) and place right side up on a wire rack. Leave to cool before serving.☐

3 **Decorating the cakes.** Gently brush the cakes to remove loose crumbs. Grate coconut (*page 26*). Warm jam—here, seedless raspberry—over a low heat. Spear the base of a cake on a fork. Using a pastry brush, paint the top and sides of the cake with jam, then roll it in the coconut. Coat the remaining cakes.

4 **Serving the cakes.** Arrange the cakes on a serving dish and garnish with halved glacé cherries, shapes cut out of marzipan (*recipe, page 45*) or angelica. To remove surface sugar from the angelica, plunge it into boiling water and leave for a minute or two. Dry on a cloth and cut it into shapes—here, diamonds. Serve the cakes.☐

Spirited Treatments for Coffee

Strong coffee, with its assertive flavour and aroma, marries well with spices, citrus fruits or spirits to create rich beverages suitable for serving at the end of a meal. *Café brûlot* (*right; recipe, page 48*) and Irish coffee (*opposite page, below; recipe, page 98*) are classic examples.

Complex mixtures such as *café brûlot* include brandy and also liqueurs such as kirsch or the curaçao used here; other flavourings can be slivered rinds of oranges and lemons as well as sugar, cinnamon and cloves. The flavourings should be crushed, then heated with the spirit and liqueur; igniting the liquid mixture before adding the coffee concentrates the flavours of the alcoholic drink.

Irish coffee is a simpler affair: it consists primarily of coffee flavoured with sugar and spirits. Irish whiskey is the traditional spirit; rum, brandy or coffee liqueur could be used instead. What gives this drink its distinction is the thick layer of cream that floats on the top. To ensure that the cream is distributed evenly and slowly over the surface of the coffee, it is poured on over the back of a spoon.

An Elaborate Blend of Brandy and Spices

1 **Peeling citrus fruit.** Prepare a pot of strong coffee; keep it warm on a fireproof mat set over a low heat or in a water bath. With a small, sharp knife, pare the rind from oranges and lemons, leaving the bitter white pith on the fruit (*above*). Slice the rind into *julienne*.

2 **Releasing the oils.** Put the orange and lemon *julienne* into a shallow pan or chafing dish, together with cubes of sugar, a cinnamon stick and cloves. Mash all the ingredients with a ladle (*above*) to release the oil from the rinds.

5 **Serving the coffee.** After a few seconds, gradually pour the prepared coffee into the pan, stirring until the flame has died out (*left*). Ladle the spiced coffee at once into small cups for serving (*above*). □

3 **Stirring the flavourings.** Add brandy and curaçao to the rinds, sugar and spices in the pan. Set the pan over a low heat, on a fireproof mat, if necessary. Stir the ingredients with the ladle (*above*) for a couple of minutes, pressing down on the sugar to help it dissolve. Stop stirring when the flavourings are thoroughly blended and the sugar is completely dissolved.

4 **Flaming the alcohol.** Continue to heat the ingredients for a few seconds more. Then light a match and pass the flame over the pan, close to the surface of the liquid, to ignite the brandy. The alcohol will burn with a blue flame (*above*).

Laced Coffee with a Blanket of Cream

1 **Pouring in whiskey.** Prepare a pot of strong coffee; keep it warm. Put a spoonful of sugar—or more to taste—into a stemmed glass with a wide bowl; then pour Irish whiskey over the sugar (*above*).

2 **Adding the coffee.** Pour the hot coffee into the glass to within about 1 cm (½ inch) of the rim (*above*)—the ratio should be about two parts coffee to one of whiskey. Stir the ingredients gently until they are blended and the sugar has dissolved.

3 **Making a layer of cream.** Rest the neck of an inverted dessertspoon on the rim of the glass so that the tip of the spoon's bowl barely touches the surface of the coffee. Gradually pour double cream over the back of the spoon, until there is a layer of cream about 5 mm (¼ inch) thick on top of the coffee (*above*).□

Anthology of Recipes

Recipes in this anthology have been selected from some of the world's best cookbooks. Introductory notes in italics and further basic recipes have been added by the *Cook in Season* Editors. Both metric and imperial measurements for each ingredient are given in separate columns. The two sets of figures are not exact equivalents, but are consistent for each recipe. Working from either metric or imperial weights and measures will produce equally good results, but the two systems should not be mixed for the same recipe. All spoon measures are level.

Fried Rice Croquettes

Arancine e Supplì di Riso

If prosciutto is not available, gammon can be substituted.

The veal, chicken livers and ham for these croquettes may be cooked separately and each rice ball filled with a different mixture, so that each will be a surprise for the taste-buds.

	To serve 6	
400 g	round-grain rice	14 oz
1	onion, thinly sliced	1
100 g	butter	3½ oz
60 cl	meat stock (*Basics booklet*), heated	1 pint
60 g	Parmesan cheese, grated	2 oz
2	eggs, beaten	2
30 g	dried mushrooms, soaked for 2 hours in at least 3 changes of warm water, drained and sliced	1 oz
100 g	lean veal, diced	3½ oz
100 g	chicken livers, diced	3½ oz
100 g	prosciutto, diced	3½ oz
	salt and pepper	
60 g	fine dry breadcrumbs	2 oz
1.25 litres	oil for frying	2 pints

Brown half of the onion in 30 g (1 oz) of the butter. Add the rice, and stir until the grains are evenly coated with butter. Gradually add 30 cl (½ pint) of the hot stock. Cover the pan and cook over a medium heat for about 15 minutes. A few minutes before the end of the cooking time, add the Parmesan cheese and 40 g (1½ oz) of the remaining butter. Stir thoroughly, then remove the rice from the heat. Leave to cool, then add the beaten eggs to the mixture.

To make the stuffing, brown the remaining onion in the rest of the butter. Add the mushrooms and simmer for a few minutes; then add the diced meats. Add half the remaining stock, season lightly with salt and pepper, and cover the pan. Cook for at least 20 minutes, or until all of the liquid has been reduced to a thick sauce, stirring occasionally, and adding up to 15 cl (¼ pint) more stock if the liquid dries up before the end of the cooking time. Leave the mixture to cool.

Shape the cooked rice into six balls or cylinders. Remove a little rice to make a hollow in each ball or cylinder, and fill the hollow with some of the meat mixture. Close up the holes with the rice taken from the hollowed-out shapes. Roll these croquettes in the breadcrumbs and quickly deep fry in hot oil until golden-brown, about 1½ minutes. Drain the croquettes on brown paper and serve.

IL MONDO IN CUCINA:
MINESTRE, ZUPPE, RISO

Rice Balls

Supplì

Supplì is the Italian name for rice croquettes containing in the centre a filling such as a slice of *mozzarella* cheese and ham or mortadella sausage. They can be made most successfully with leftover *risotto*, and are so good that when making a *risotto* it is worth cooking enough to have some left over for *supplì*.

	To serve 4 to 6	
About 500 g	leftover cooked round-grain rice, or *risotto (right, above)*	About 1 lb
2	eggs, lightly beaten	2
100 g	ham, thinly sliced and cut into small squares	3½ oz
100 g	*mozzarella* cheese, thinly sliced and cut into small squares	3½ oz
	fine breadcrumbs	
	oil or fat	

Stir the eggs into the cooked rice to bind it. Take about 1 tablespoon of the rice and put it flat on the palm of your hand; on the rice, lay a little slice of ham and one of cheese. Place another tablespoon of rice on the top of the ham and cheese and form the mixture into a ball the size of a small orange, so that the ham and the cheese are completely enclosed. Roll each *supplì* very carefully in fine breadcrumbs, then fry them in hot oil or fat, turning them over and round, so that the whole of the outside is nicely browned. Drain them on brown or kitchen paper. The cheese inside should be just melted, stretching into threads as one cuts into the rice, so a hard cheese such as Gruyère is not suitable.

ELIZABETH DAVID
ITALIAN FOOD

Risotto

To serve 4 to 6

500 g	round-grain rice	1 lb
1	small onion, finely chopped	1
75 g	butter	2½ oz
About 1.25 litres	stock (*Basics booklet*)	About 2 pints
60 to 90 g	Parmesan cheese, grated	2 to 3 oz

In a shallow pan, sauté the chopped onion in 30 g (1 oz) of the butter until golden. Stir in the rice and, after a few minutes, about 15 cl (¼ pint) of the stock. With the heat on low, continue to stir the mixture slowly until the liquid is almost absorbed, then add more stock. Continue stirring and adding stock each time the liquid is absorbed, until the rice is tender but still firm to the bite. Take the pan off the heat and stir in the rest of the butter and the Parmesan cheese. Stir and serve, with more Parmesan cheese if you wish.

Forcemeat

For additional colour and flavour, chopped parboiled spinach and celery can be added to this recipe, as shown on page 7.

To make about 1 kg (2 to 2½ lb)

350 g	veal, chopped	12 oz
350 g	pork, chopped	12 oz
350 g	pork back fat, chopped	12 oz
150 g	pig's liver	5 oz
2	chicken livers, chopped (optional)	2
2	eggs	2
60 g	fresh breadcrumbs (optional)	2 oz
1	onion, finely chopped, stewed in a little butter until soft	1
1	garlic clove, finely chopped	1
1 tbsp	chopped parsley	1 tbsp
2 tbsp	brandy, Madeira, pastis, sherry, port or wine (optional)	2 tbsp
	mixed dried herbs	
	mixed spices	
	salt and pepper	

In a bowl, combine all the chopped meats; add the eggs and breadcrumbs, if using. Add the remaining ingredients and squeeze the mixture through your fingers until everything is thoroughly combined.

Terrine of Whatever You Like

Gâteau de Viande de ce que l'On Veut

The technique of lining a terrine with back fat is demonstrated on page 2.

To make 4 kg (9 lb)

2 kg	boneless lean beef, or boned leg of lamb or mutton, or boneless lean veal, or 1 hare, boned, or a mixture of these meats	4 lb
250 g	beef suet or marrow, chopped	8 oz
250 g	raw ham	8 oz
	salt	
	mixed spices	
1 tbsp	chopped parsley	1 tbsp
2	Welsh onions, chopped	2
250 g	mushrooms, finely chopped	8 oz
½ tbsp	powdered dried basil	½ tbsp
8	egg yolks	8
10 cl	*eau-de-vie* or brandy	3½ fl oz
1 kg	pork back fat, diced	2 to 2½ lb
250 g	pork back fat, sliced into thin sheets	8 oz

Chop or mince the meat with the beef suet or marrow and the ham. Season with salt, mixed spices, parsley, Welsh onions, mushrooms and basil. Add the egg yolks, *eau-de-vie* or brandy and the diced back fat; work the mixture well until it is thoroughly amalgamated.

Line a large round casserole with the thin slices of back fat, pack in the meat mixture and cover with more slices. Cover the casserole with the lid and bake the terrine in a preheated 180°C (350°F or Mark 4) oven for 4 hours, reducing the heat to 130°C (250°F or Mark ½) after the first hour. Place a weighted board on top of the meat and leave to cool.

To serve, turn the terrine out of the casserole on to a platter and scrape the covering of fat until it is uniformly white.

MENON
LES SOUPERS DE LA COUR

Pork and Spinach Loaf

Caillette Valentinoise

The technique of lining a terrine with caul is demonstrated on page 3.

To make 2 kg (4 lb)

1 kg	boned pig's head, fat and lean	2 to 2½ lb
500 g	pig's liver	1 lb
500 g	boned loin of pork	1 lb
	salt and pepper	
3	garlic cloves	3
250 g	spinach	8 oz
1	small savoy cabbage, quartered and cored	1
1	sprig parsley	1
1	egg	1
	grated nutmeg	
125 g	pork caul	4 oz
30 g	butter	1 oz
1	thin slice pork fat, 3 cm (1¼ inch) square	1
1	small branch dried sage	1

Place the pig's head in a saucepan, cover with water and add salt, pepper and one garlic clove. Bring to the boil and simmer until the meat is tender, about 2 hours. Remove the meat from the cooking liquid.

Cook the spinach and cabbage in the cooking liquid until they are tender, about 15 minutes for the cabbage and 5 minutes for the spinach. Drain each, pressing to extract excess liquid. Reserve the cooking liquid.

Chop together the cooked meat and vegetables with the liver and pork loin. Chop the two remaining garlic cloves with the parsley and add to the mixture. Add the egg and season with salt, pepper and nutmeg. Mix well. Spread the pork caul in a large dish; put in the meat mixture, mounding it up, and wrap the edges of the caul round it to enclose it completely.

Pour 45 cl (¾ pint) of the cooking liquid into a baking dish. Put in the butter and turn the wrapped meat mixture into the baking dish so that the edges of the caul are underneath. In the middle, place the pork fat, secured with the branch of sage. Place in a preheated 190°C (375°F or Mark 5) oven and bake, uncovered, for 1 hour. Baste regularly with the pan juices and the remaining cooking liquid after the first 30 minutes; make sure that the loaf does not dry out. This dish may be eaten either hot or cold.

PAUL BOUILLARD
LA CUISINE AU COIN DU FEU

Sausage Balls from the Ardèche

Caillettes de l'Ardèche

To prepare caul, see the demonstration on page 3.

To make 1 kg (2 to 2½ lb)

500 g	sausage-meat	1 lb
500 g	Swiss chard, blanched	1 lb
100 g	spinach, blanched	3½ oz
1	stick celery, blanched	1
150 g	pig's liver	5 oz
	salt and pepper	
	quatre épices	
	dried thyme	
	dried basil	
125 g	pork caul	4 oz

Chop together all the blanched vegetables and the pig's liver. Mix with the sausage-meat, season with salt, pepper, *quatre épices*, thyme and basil and blend well.

Form small balls of the mixture and wrap them in pieces of caul. Place in a buttered baking dish and bake in a preheated 220°C (425°F or Mark 7) oven for about 20 minutes. These are served either very hot, with mashed potatoes—or cold.

EUGÉNIE BRAZIER
LES SECRETS DE LA MÈRE BRAZIER

Faggots

Gayettes

To prepare caul, see the demonstration on page 3.

To make 1.25 kg (2½ lb)

250 g	pig's liver, diced	8 oz
250 g	calf's lungs, diced	8 oz
300 g	pig's kidney, diced	10 oz
300 g	sausage-meat	10 oz
100 g	chicken livers, minced	3½ oz
	salt and pepper	
1	garlic clove	1
1	shallot, chopped	1
3 tbsp	chopped parsley	3 tbsp
1	truffle (optional), diced	1
125 g	pork caul, cut into squares	4 oz

Place in a bowl the pig's liver, the lungs, kidney, salt and pepper, garlic, shallot, parsley and the truffle if using. Cover and leave to marinate for 10 to 12 hours.

Chop the marinated mixture roughly; add the sausage-meat and chicken livers. Form the mixture into balls the size of tangerines and wrap each ball in a piece of caul. Place in a greased baking dish and cook in a preheated 180°C (350°F or Mark 4) oven for 1½ hours. Serve cold.

70 MÉDECINS DE FRANCE
LE TRÉSOR DE LA CUISINE DU BASSIN MÉDITERRANÉEN

Mussels "Poulette"

The techniques of cleaning and steaming mussels are demonstrated on page 8.

To serve 8 to 10

3 litres	live mussels, scrubbed clean and soaked in salted water for 30 minutes	5 pints
1	stick celery, chopped	1
1	bay leaf	1
2 tbsp	chopped flat-leafed parsley	2 tbsp
2	sprigs thyme	2
2	garlic cloves, crushed	2
	dry white wine	
6	egg yolks	6
20 cl	double cream	7 fl oz

Put the mussels in a large pan, add the celery, bay leaf, parsley, thyme and garlic and pour in a generous splash of white wine. Cover the pan and open the mussels over a high heat, shaking the pan often until all the mussels have opened—3 to 5 minutes. Line a colander with several layers of dampened muslin, then tip the mussels into the colander. Taste the liquid for salt: if it is not salty, reduce it by boiling. If it is very salty do not reduce it, but use only part of it to make the sauce. The remainder can be used to make soup or stock.

Once the mussels are cool enough to touch, pull the shells apart, discarding each empty half shell. Arrange the mussels in their half shells in a large shallow pan. Whisk the egg yolks with the cream and gradually whisk in 10 to 15 cl (3½ to 5 fl oz) of the cooking liquid. Pour this mixture over the mussels. Place the pan over a gentle heat, shaking it gently from side to side until the sauce thickens—about 10 minutes. Make sure that the sauce does not boil whilst it is thickening. Ladle the mussels and sauce into soup plates and serve immediately.

PETITS PROPOS CULINAIRES 11

Gratin of Hard-Boiled Eggs in Creamed Sorrel

Gratin d'Oeufs Durs à la Crème d'Oseille

The prevent the sorrel from discolouring, use a non-reactive pan to make the purée.

To serve 4 to 6

6	eggs, hard-boiled and halved	6
300 g	sorrel	10 oz
	salt and pepper	
125 g	butter	4 oz
40 g	fresh breadcrumbs	1½ oz
¼ litre	double cream	8 fl oz

If the sorrel is young and tender, cut it into fine shreds and stew it gently, salted, in 40 g (1½ oz) of the butter. If older, plunge the leaves first into boiling water, drain them the moment the water returns to the boil and then stew in 40 g (1½ oz) of butter, stirring regularly, for about 20 minutes or until the liquid has evaporated and the sorrel has melted into a purée. Stir in the cream a little at a time, permitting it to absorb the sorrel and thicken before adding more; grind in some pepper and taste for salt.

While the sorrel is stewing, put the breadcrumbs to cook in the remaining butter over a low heat, stirring or tossing regularly until they are lightly golden.

Butter a gratin dish just large enough to hold the eggs. Arrange the eggs, cut surface up, side by side. Spoon the hot sauce over them, evenly masking all the eggs. Sprinkle the sautéed breadcrumbs regularly over the entire surface, and bake in an oven preheated to 200°C (400°F or Mark 6) for about 15 minutes or until the gratin is well heated through and the surface is lightly browned.

RICHARD OLNEY
SIMPLE FRENCH FOOD

Creamed Spinach

	To serve 4 to 6	
1 kg	spinach, stemmed	2 to 2½ lb
30 g	butter	1 oz
12.5 cl	double cream	4 fl oz
	salt and pepper	
	grated nutmeg	

Bring a large pot of water to the boil, plunge in the spinach, and parboil for 2 minutes. Drain the spinach in a colander, running cold water over it to stop the cooking. With your hands, squeeze out excess moisture. Chop the spinach. Over a medium heat, melt the butter and stir in the chopped spinach. Stir until any excess moisture has evaporated. Reduce the heat. Stir in the double cream. Season to taste with the salt, pepper and a little grated nutmeg.

Eggs in Onion Sauce

Oeufs à la Tripe

The French title of this dish indicates its similarity in texture to tripe and onions. To give the sauce extra body and colour, two or three raw egg yolks and a tablespoon of chopped parsley may be stirred in just before the sliced eggs are added.

	To serve 6	
12	eggs, hard-boiled and sliced into rounds	12
6	onions, thinly sliced	6
125 g	butter	4 oz
	salt and pepper	
1 tbsp	flour	1 tbsp
¼ litre	single cream or rich milk	8 fl oz

In a saucepan, melt the butter, add the onions, and season them with salt and pepper. Cook over a low heat until the onions are soft and golden, but not browned—8 to 10 minutes. Sprinkle on the flour, and pour in the cream or milk. Turn up the heat to bring the sauce to the boil, then reduce the heat at once and cook, stirring, for 25 to 30 minutes. Add the sliced eggs and heat them briefly in the sauce without allowing the mixture to boil. Serve very hot.

JULES BRETEUIL
LE CUISINIER EUROPÉEN

Hard-Boiled Eggs Villemont

Oeufs Durs Villemont

	To serve 4	
8	eggs	8
75 g	butter	2½ oz
300 g	onions, halved and thinly sliced, blanched for 5 minutes if strong flavoured	10 oz
½	sweet red pepper, cut into thin strips	½
50 g	Swiss chard leaves, coarsely chopped	2 oz
1½ tbsp	flour	1½ tbsp
10 cl	tepid milk	3½ fl oz
	salt and pepper	
	grated nutmeg	
15 cl	double cream	¼ pint

For the sauce, heat the butter in a sauté pan. Add the onions and pepper and fry gently for 5 minutes, stirring. Cover the pan and sweat the vegetables over a low heat for 15 minutes. Add the chard and cook for 5 minutes without browning. Sprinkle with the flour. Cook for a few moments, stirring. Add the warm milk little by little and stir briskly to ensure that the sauce does not lump. Season with salt, pepper and a pinch of nutmeg. Simmer very gently for 20 minutes. Add the cream, return the sauce to the boil, and adjust the seasoning.

While the sauce is cooking, place the eggs carefully in a sieve and immerse them in a large pan of boiling salted water. Cook them for 9 minutes, then run them under cold water until they are cool enough to be handled. Shell them and place them in a pan of warm, slightly salted, water.

To serve, cut the eggs in half and arrange them in a heatproof dish. Cover with the sauce, reheat for 1 or 2 minutes over a low heat, and serve.

JEAN AND PIERRE TROISGROS
CUISINIERS À ROANNE

Roast Mallard

Malars de Rivière

The bird can be roasted for 15 minutes in a preheated 230°C (450°F or Mark 8) oven instead of over an open fire. The legs should then be removed and grilled for a further 10 minutes. Another method for cooking the sauce, suggested by the author, is to put the onions in the drip pan as explained and, when the bird is cooked, to add the juice of a lemon and 4 tablespoons each of wine and wine vinegar to the drip pan. Boil the mixture and add the toast. This sauce is called saupiquet.

To serve 2

1	young mallard, drawn and trussed	1
2	onions, coarsely chopped	2
60 g	green streaky bacon, diced	2 oz
1 tbsp	chopped parsley	1 tbsp
1	slice toast, crusts removed, crumbled	1
	coarse salt	

Thread the duck on to a spit over an open fire. Put the onions underneath in a drip pan so they will cook in the juices from the bird. When the bird is cooked, put the bacon and parsley in the pan and add the toast. Put the pan over a medium heat and cook until the bacon is lightly browned. Untruss the duck and serve with the onion and toast mixture.

LE MÉNAGIER DE PARIS

Roast Grouse

The technique of removing the legs is demonstrated on page 15.

To serve 4

4	grouse, trussed	4
4	pieces pork back fat, 5 mm (¼ inch thick)	2
	salt and pepper	
	watercress, to garnish	
	bread sauce (*right*)	

Tie one piece of back fat to each grouse, so that it covers the breast. Season the birds with salt and pepper. Place them in a roasting pan and put them into an oven preheated to 230°C (450°F or Mark 8) for about 15 minutes. Remove the barding fat and roast the grouse for a further 5 minutes or until the breasts are lightly browned. Cut and remove the trussing string. Cut the legs away and keep them for stock or another dish. Place the birds on a serving dish and garnish with watercress. Serve with bread sauce.

Farce Gratin

A *farce gratin*, a traditional garnish for game birds, uses game bird livers, often with additional poultry livers to make up the desired weight. The proportion of poultry to game bird livers should be about one to four for small game birds; for pheasant, use one poultry liver to two pheasant livers.

To make 200 g (7 oz)

150 g	game livers or game and poultry livers, trimmed	5 oz
2 or 3	shallots, finely chopped	2 or 3
30 g	butter	1 oz
	salt and pepper	
2 tbsp	brandy	2 tbsp

Gently stew the shallots in the butter for about 5 minutes without letting them colour. Add the livers, season with salt and pepper, increase the heat and cook for 2 minutes, stirring continually. Pour in the brandy, set it alight and remove from the heat. Stir until the flames die down.

Allow the mixture to cool until tepid. Pour the contents of the pan, including the juices, into a mortar or food processor. Pound or purée the mixture, then force it through a sieve.

Bread Sauce

To make the sauce thicker, whisk in a few fresh breadcrumbs after removing the onion and seasonings. If a thinner consistency is preferred, add more cream.

To make ½ litre (16 fl oz)

100 g	crustless fresh white bread, crumbled	3½ oz
60 cl	milk	1 pint
1	onion, stuck with 2 cloves	1
	salt	
1	bay leaf	1
1	blade mace	1
10 cl	double cream	3½ fl oz
30 g	butter, cut into pieces	1 oz

Pour the milk into a saucepan, add the onion, a pinch of salt, the bay leaf and mace and bring the milk to the boil. Stir in the bread and reduce the heat. Simmer the milk over a low heat for about 20 minutes, stirring occasionally, to flavour it with the onion and seasonings. Remove the onion and seasonings with a slotted spoon and whisk the cream into the sauce. Remove the pan from the heat and whisk in the butter.

Hottish Barbecue Sauce

This sauce is ideal as an accompaniment to grilled spareribs and will keep well in the refrigerator.

To make 60 cl (1 pint)

4	garlic cloves	4
1 tbsp	salt	1 tbsp
¼ litre	olive oil	8 fl oz
12.5 cl	vinegar	4 fl oz
1	small onion, finely chopped	1
1	small sweet green pepper, finely chopped	1
1 tbsp	chili powder	1 tbsp
¼ litre	tomato juice	8 fl oz
1 tsp	oregano	1 tsp

Crush the garlic with the salt. Add the oil, vinegar, onion, green pepper, chili powder, tomato juice and oregano. Simmer this mixture for 10 minutes and strain before using.

HELEN BROWN
HELEN BROWN'S WEST COAST COOK BOOK

Sweet-and-Sour Spareribs

For more flavour, the ribs can be salted down overnight with a salt and herb mixture (recipe, page 42).

To serve 6

1 kg	rack pork spareribs, fat trimmed	2 to 2½ lb
1	chili pepper, seeded and chopped	1
1	clove garlic, crushed	1
1 tsp	mustard powder	1 tsp
1 tsp	mixed herbs	1 tsp
½	orange, juice only	½
3 to 4 tbsp	wine vinegar	3 to 4 tbsp
3 to 4 tbsp	honey	3 to 4 tbsp
1 tbsp	olive oil	1 tbsp
1	onion, finely chopped	1
500 g	can plum tomatoes	1 lb

Pound the chili, garlic, mustard and herbs in a mortar. Add the orange juice, vinegar and honey, stir thoroughly and sieve into a bowl. Stew the onion in the oil until soft. Drain the canned tomatoes, sieve them and add them to the onions. Pour in the sieved chili sauce and bring to the boil, stirring continuously. Lower the heat and simmer the sauce for about 30 minutes or until it has reduced by half. Place the ribs in a roasting pan and roast in a preheated oven at 200°C (400°F or Mark 6) for 10 minutes. Take out of the oven and remove the exuded fat.

Lower the temperature to 180°C (350°F or Mark 4). Ladle some of the sauce over the ribs to coat them thickly and return the pan to the oven for about 45 minutes, basting at 10-minute intervals with the sauce and pan juices. Add extra sauce if the pan dries out. The sauce should form a thick glaze on the ribs. Remove from the oven and carve.

Barbecued Spareribs

The technique of cooking marinated spareribs on a grill is demonstrated on page 17.

To serve 6

1 kg	rack pork spareribs, left whole, fat trimmed, cut between each rib but not separated	2½ lb
	salt and sugar (optional)	
2 tbsp	honey (optional)	2 tbsp
1 tsp	soy sauce (optional)	1 tsp
	Marinade	
1	garlic clove, crushed	1
3	slices fresh ginger root, crushed	3
¼ litre	soy sauce	8 fl oz
1 tbsp	sugar	1 tbsp
1 tbsp	sherry	1 tbsp

Before marinating, the rib rack may be rubbed with salt and sugar and left for 1 hour.

Combine the crushed garlic and ginger with the soy sauce, sugar and sherry and rub the marinade over the ribs and into the cuts as well. Place the ribs in a shallow pan and pour the rest of the marinade over them. Let stand 2 to 4 hours at room temperature, basting and turning meat from time to time. (Do not marinate for a longer period: the meat will toughen.) Drain, reserving marinade.

Preheat the oven to 190°C (375°F or Mark 5). Place the ribs on a metal rack over a roasting pan nearly filled with water to catch the drippings and keep them from burning. Or suspend the ribs high in the oven over the drip pan. Roast for about 45 minutes, basting frequently with the reserved marinade. If ribs are roasted flat, they should be turned at 15 to 20 minute intervals for even browning. Half way through cooking, the ribs may be glazed with the combined honey and soy sauce.

The heat may be turned up to 230°C (450°F or Mark 8) during the last 5 minutes of roasting to crisp the ribs, but any longer tends to dry them out. To barbecue ribs on a charcoal grill, prepare as above, but increase amount of marinade and baste more frequently to keep the ribs from drying out.

GLORIA BLEY MILLER
THE THOUSAND RECIPE CHINESE COOKBOOK

Veal Patties with Sour Cream Sauce

Fricadelles de Veau Smitane

You can have the meat minced by your butcher, but it is better if you chop it by hand with a pair of big knives (page 18).

To serve 6

600 g	veal tenderloin, trimmed and chopped	1¼ lb
30 cl	double cream	½ pint
90 g	fresh white breadcrumbs	3 oz
⅛ tsp	freshly grated nutmeg	⅛ tsp
½ tsp	freshly ground white pepper	½ tsp
1 tsp	salt	1 tsp
40 g	unsalted butter	1½ oz
1½ tbsp	vegetable oil	1½ tbsp
	Sauce	
15 g	unsalted butter	½ oz
90 g	onion, finely chopped	3 oz
¼ tsp	crushed black peppercorns	¼ tsp
1	bay leaf	1
5 tbsp	white wine vinegar	5 tbsp
1 tsp	flour	1 tsp
30 cl	double cream	½ pint
¾ tsp	salt	¾ tsp

Place the chopped meat in a clean vessel (not aluminium) over ice. The meat must be very cold. Mix 15 cl (¼ pint) of the cream with half the breadcrumbs to make a paste and set this aside. Start adding the remaining cream to the meat, 1 tablespoon at a time, beating with a wooden spatula after each addition so that the cream is well incorporated into the meat. Keep adding the cream until it is all used. Add the nutmeg, pepper and salt. (You will notice that the salt will tighten the mixture after it is added. This is why it is added only at the end.) Mix in the bread and cream mixture. Spread the remaining breadcrumbs on the table. Separate the mixture into six patties and flatten each into a round about 10 cm (4 inches) in diameter and 2 cm (¾ inch) thick. Dip them into the breadcrumbs on both sides. Set the patties aside.

To make the sauce, melt the butter in a saucepan, add the onion, peppercorns and bay leaf, and sauté on a low heat for about 8 minutes, until the onions are a golden colour. Stir in the vinegar and reduce until the onions are only just moist. Sprinkle with the flour, mix with a spoon and add the cream. Bring to the boil, stirring to avoid scorching. Add salt and reduce to about 20 cl (7 fl oz), until nice and smooth. Strain the sauce through a fine-meshed sieve and set aside.

Heat the butter and oil in a large skillet. When hot, place the *fricadelles* flat in the fat. Reduce the heat to low and cook for about 5 to 6 minutes on each side, or until nicely browned.

Arrange on a serving platter and coat with the sauce.

JACQUES PÉPIN
A FRENCH CHEF COOKS AT HOME

Nutty Grilled Hamburgers

Polpette di Carne alla Griglia

To serve 4 to 6

750 g	beef, minced	1½ lb
1	medium-sized onion, chopped	1
1	large garlic clove, finely chopped	1
60 g	breadcrumbs	2 oz
60 g	Romano cheese, or Parmesan cheese, grated	2 oz
125 g	pine-nuts	4 oz
8 tbsp	chopped parsley	8 tbsp
2	eggs	2
1½ tsp	salt	1½ tsp
1 tsp	freshly ground black pepper	1 tsp
	oil	

Preheat the grill. Combine the beef, onion, garlic, breadcrumbs, cheese, pine-nuts, parsley, eggs, salt and pepper; mix well. Shape the mixture into thick, 5 to 6 cm (2½ inch), rounds.

Brush the grilling rack with oil and grill 7.5 cm (3 inches) from the heat source for about 5 minutes on each side or until the hamburgers are well browned and crispy.

ANNA MUFFOLETTO
THE ART OF SICILIAN COOKING

Dry-Salting Mixture for Meat

This amount of salting mixture is sufficient for about 2 kg (4 lb) of meat. For larger quantities of meat, proportionately less of the mixture will be needed.

	To make 500 g (1 lb)	
500 g	coarse salt	1 lb
4	allspice berries	4
4	cloves	4
6	juniper berries	6
2	bay leaves	2
6	peppercorns	6
1 tbsp	mixed dried herbs	1 tbsp

In a mortar, crush the allspice, cloves, juniper berries, bay leaves and peppercorns together coarsely. Mix with the salt and herbs. Rub the salt mixture over the meat to be salted, ensuring that it is evenly covered. Put a layer of the salt mixture in the bottom of the bowl or crock you are using, put in the salted pieces of meat, and sprinkle a generous quantity of the mixture over the top.

Abdullah Beef

Boeuf Abdullah

	To serve 4	
500 g	beef, minced	1 lb
1	medium-sized onion, chopped	1
125 g	butter	4 oz
1	egg	1
2	thick slices day-old bread, crusts removed, soaked in milk and squeezed	2
	salt and pepper	
	toasted white breadcrumbs	
¼ litre	yogurt	8 fl oz
60 g	mushrooms, chopped	2 oz

In a large frying pan, fry the onion in some of the butter until transparent. Remove from the heat and cool a little. Mix well together the meat, onion, egg, bread and seasoning. Shape into small balls, flatten slightly, roll in the breadcrumbs and brown slowly in butter. Add the remaining butter to the pan as needed. Add the yogurt and mushrooms and simmer for 30 minutes. Serve hot.

IRFAN ORGA
COOKING WITH YOGURT

Fried Meat Balls

Keftedes Tiganites

	To make about 24	
500 g	lean beef or veal, minced	1 lb
1	medium-sized onion, finely chopped	1
1	garlic clove, crushed (optional)	1
2	slices bread, crusts removed, soaked in water and squeezed dry	2
1	egg, lightly beaten	1
3 tbsp	chopped fresh parsley	3 tbsp
2	sprigs fresh mint, chopped	2
½ tsp	ground allspice, cinnamon or coriander	½ tsp
1 tbsp	dry red wine	1 tbsp
2 to 3 tbsp	water, if necessary	2 to 3 tbsp
	salt and freshly ground pepper	
	flour	
	vegetable oil	

In a mixing bowl, combine the meat with the onion, garlic, bread, egg, parsley, mint, spice and wine, then knead for 2 minutes. The mixture should be soft; add water if necessary. Season with salt and pepper to taste, then cover and refrigerate for at least 1 hour. Pinch off small portions the size of walnuts or smaller and roll into balls between your palms, then dredge lightly in flour. Pour oil into a frying pan to a depth of 1 cm (½ inch) and heat the oil until it reaches the smoking point. Slip in the *keftedes* and fry until crisp, turning constantly with tongs. Remove with a slotted spoon and drain on absorbent paper.

VILMA LIACOURAS CHANTILES
THE FOOD OF GREECE

Quinces Stuffed with Beef or Veal

Dyuli, Pulneni s Meso

This dish is best when made with lean meat chopped by hand, as demonstrated on page 18.

	To serve 8	
8	ripe quinces, tops (stalk end) cut off and reserved	8
400 g	beef or veal, minced	14 oz
50 g	onion, finely chopped	2 oz
10 cl	oil, or 100 g (3½ oz) butter	3½ fl oz
1 tsp	paprika	1 tsp
¼ tsp	ground cinnamon	¼ tsp
	salt	
	hot beef or veal stock (*Basics booklet*), or water	
1 to 2 tsp	sugar	1 to 2 tsp
8 cl	tomato juice	3 fl oz
2	egg yolks, whisked	2

With a small, sharp knife and a sturdy spoon, remove the cores and seeds from the quinces, leaving the base of each fruit intact. Make sure any hard parts surrounding the core are also scraped away, leaving an opening large enough to contain the meat filling.

To prepare the stuffing, brown the chopped onion in the oil or butter, then add the minced meat, together with the paprika, ground cinnamon and a little salt. Stir-fry the mixture until most of the pan juices have evaporated. Taste and adjust the seasonings, if necessary. Fill the quinces with this mixture, put their lids on, and place them, standing upright, in an ovenproof dish or pan large enough to hold them in a single layer. Pour in meat stock or water until it comes one-third of the way up the sides of the quinces, then add the sugar and tomato juice, seasoned with a little salt.

Cook the dish on top of the stove, covered, on a medium heat for about 30 minutes, or bake in a preheated 180°C (350°F or Mark 4) oven for about 45 minutes. The quinces are ready when quite soft but not disintegrating, and the pan juices have reduced to less than half their original volume.

To serve, place the quinces on individual dinner plates and keep warm. Strain the pan juices and add gradually to the egg yolks, whisking all the time. Then pour this sauce into a small saucepan and place over a low heat until heated through but not boiling. Pour equal amounts of sauce over each fruit and serve immediately.

M. TSOLOVA, V. STOILOVA AND SN. EKIMOVA
IZPOLZOUVANE NA ZELENCHOUTSITE I PLODOVETE V DOMAKINSTVOTO

Stuffed Papaya

The technique of stuffing papayas is demonstrated on page 22. The author recommends serving the papaya with tomato sauce. To make the tomato sauce, fry a finely chopped onion in 1 tablespoonful of olive oil until the onion is soft but not brown. Add 750 g (1½ lb) of chopped, ripe tomatoes; two chopped garlic cloves; 1 teaspoon of dried thyme; a chopped bay leaf, and, if you wish, 1 to 2 teaspoons of sugar. Season with salt and pepper and simmer for 20 to 30 minutes or until the tomatoes are reduced to a thick pulp. Before serving, sieve the sauce, using a pestle or wooden spoon to push it through the sieve.

	To serve 6	
500 g	underripe papayas, peeled, halved and seeded	1 lb
2 tbsp	oil	2 tbsp
1	large onion, finely chopped	1
1	garlic clove, chopped	1
500 g	lean beef, minced	1 lb
3	medium-sized tomatoes, skinned and chopped	3
1	red or green chili pepper, seeded and chopped	1
	salt and pepper	
4 tbsp	grated Parmesan cheese	4 tbsp
15 g	unsalted butter, cut into small pieces	½ oz

Drop the papaya halves into boiling, salted water and parboil them for 10 minutes. Drain the papayas thoroughly and pat them dry with kitchen paper. Heat the oil in a frying pan and add the onion, garlic and minced beef. Sauté for 15 minutes, stirring from time to time to break up the meat. Add the tomatoes, chili pepper and salt and pepper to taste and cook for a few minutes, stirring until the mixture is well blended and thick. Arrange the papaya halves in a greased baking tin and fill them with the meat mixture. Sprinkle with the grated cheese and dot with the pieces of butter. Bake in a preheated 180°C (350°F or Mark 4) oven for 30 to 40 minutes or until the papayas are completely tender.

ELISABETH LAMBERT ORTIZ
CARIBBEAN COOKING

Caramel Custard

Crème Caramel Renversée à la Vanille

The technique of caramelizing a mould is shown on page 24.

	To serve 3	
2	eggs	2
2	egg yolks	2
2 tsp	castor sugar	2 tsp
About $\frac{1}{2}$ tsp	vanilla extract	About $\frac{1}{2}$ tsp
	salt	
30 cl	milk	$\frac{1}{2}$ pint
	Caramel	
90 g	granulated sugar	3 oz
5 tbsp	cold water	5 tbsp
1 tsp	lemon juice	1 tsp

Put the ingredients for the caramel into a small tin-lined saucepan, and let them cook until they are a light coffee colour. Watch the caramel carefully, as it is apt to burn. When it is ready, pour it into a plain, dry, 60 cl (1 pint) soufflé mould which has straight sides and a flat bottom, and turn the mould round and round until the caramel coats it uniformly. It is a good plan to warm the mould first. Allow the caramel to become cold whilst making the custard.

Put the eggs and egg yolks into a basin with the castor sugar, vanilla extract to taste and a pinch of salt, and mix them to a cream with a wooden spoon. Heat the milk, and pour it slowly on to the egg mixture, stirring all the time. Strain the custard into the prepared mould and cover with greased paper. Steam *very* slowly for about an hour until the custard feels firm in the centre; or bake in an oven preheated to 170° to 180°C (325° to 350°F or Mark 3 to 4), with some warm water round the mould. Let the custard stand until tepid before turning it out. The pudding will have a glaze of caramel over the top, and some of the caramel will run round the sides as a sauce. Serve tepid, or chill and serve cold.

FLORENCE B. JACK
COOKERY FOR EVERY HOUSEHOLD

Alison's Orange Caramel Custard

Pudin de Naranjas

The technique of caramelizing a mould is shown on page 24.

	To serve 6 to 8	
250 g	sugar	8 oz
30 g	butter	1 oz
30 g	flour	1 oz
6	eggs, yolks separated from whites	6
30 cl	orange juice	$\frac{1}{2}$ pint

Caramelize 100 g (3$\frac{1}{2}$ oz) of the sugar in a heavy pan. Pour the caramel into a 90 cl (1$\frac{1}{2}$ pint), round, ovenproof glass dish, and tip the dish so that the bottom and sides are evenly coated with the caramel. Cream the butter with the remaining sugar. Add the flour and mix well. Beat the egg yolks very well, and add them to the butter mixture, then add the orange juice. Beat the egg whites until stiff and fold them into the mixture. Pour the mixture into the caramel-lined dish, set the dish in a pan of hot water and bake in an oven preheated to 180°C (350°F or Mark 4) for 1 hour. Turn the dessert out on to a serving dish so that the caramel glaze is on top. Serve the custard hot and, if you wish, flaming with brandy or rum.

HELEN BROWN
HELEN BROWN'S WEST COAST COOK BOOK

Macaroon Custard

Bonet

The technique of caramelizing a mould is shown on page 24.

	To serve 3 or 4	
50 g	macaroons, crumbled	2 oz
4	egg yolks	4
100 g	sugar	3$\frac{1}{2}$ oz
1 tbsp	cocoa	1 tbsp
1 tbsp	rum	1 tbsp
$\frac{1}{4}$ litre	milk	8 fl oz
2 to 3 tbsp	water	2 to 3 tbsp

In a mixing bowl, beat the egg yolks with 4 tablespoons of the sugar. When the mixture is pale and creamy, add the crumbled macaroons, the cocoa, rum and milk, beating with a whisk until all the ingredients are well blended.

Dissolve the remaining sugar in the water, and cook over a moderate heat until the sugar caramelizes. Coat the base and sides of a 60 cl (1 pint) pudding mould with the caramel, then pour in the custard mixture. Put the mould into a pan filled with very hot, almost boiling water to come half way up the height of the mould. Cook in a preheated, 170°C (325°F or Mark 3) oven for 1 hour. Take care that the water does not boil.

When the custard is set, remove it from the oven, set it aside for 10 minutes, then unmould it on to a plate. The custard can be served hot or cold.

LAURA GRAS PORTINARI
CUCINA E VINI DEL PIEMONTE E DELLA VALLE D'AOSTA

Marzipan

To make 750 g (1½ lb)

350 g	ground almonds	12 oz
350 g	icing sugar, sifted	12 oz
½	lemon, juice strained	½
2	egg whites, lightly beaten	2

Mix together the ground almonds and icing sugar in a bowl. Make a well in the centre and add the lemon juice and some of the egg white. Mix them into the dry ingredients with a knife, then work the mixture by hand until it starts to come away from the sides of the bowl. Stir in enough of the remaining egg white to make a stiff paste. Turn the paste out on to a marble slab lightly sprinkled with icing sugar and knead it gently until smooth. Do not overwork the paste or it will become oily.

Praline

To make 500 g (1 lb)

250 g	almonds, blanched	8 oz
250 g	sugar	8 oz
	almond oil	

Place the almonds and sugar in a heavy pan over a very low heat; stir continually until the nuts are toasted and the sugar has caramelized and is a pale amber. Pour the mixture on to a marble slab lightly oiled with almond oil, and spread it out to form a thin layer over the slab. Leave it to cool completely.

When the praline is cold and hard, break it into pieces and remove it from the slab. Place the pieces in a large plastic bag and pound them into coarse crumbs with a rolling pin. Sift the crumbs through a coarse-meshed sieve. Return any larger pieces that will not go through the sieve to the plastic bag and repeat until all the nut mixture is powdered.

White Praline

To make about 350 g (12 oz)

175 g	sugar	6 oz
5 tbsp	water	5 tbsp
175 g	ground almonds	6 oz
	almond oil	

In a heavy saucepan, dissolve the sugar in the water over a very low heat. Bring to the boil and cook the syrup until it reaches the hard-ball stage (*Basics booklet*). Take the pan off the heat and thoroughly stir in the ground almonds. Oil a marble slab lightly with almond oil and pour the mixture out on to the slab. Spread it out to form a thin layer on the slab and allow it to cool completely. When it is cold and hard, break the praline into pieces and press it through a coarse-meshed metal sieve to make a fine powder.

Chocolate Frosting

To make 500 g (1 lb)

100 g	hard bitter chocolate	3½ oz
40 g	butter, cut into cubes	1½ oz
300 g	icing sugar, sifted	10 oz
	salt	
1 tsp	vanilla extract or 1 tbsp vanilla sugar	1 tsp
5 tbsp	milk	5 tbsp

Melt the chocolate and butter together in a pan over a low heat, stirring all the time. Keep the pan on the heat while you stir in the icing sugar, a pinch of salt and the vanilla extract or vanilla sugar. Pour in the milk and stir it in. Beat the mixture in the pan, over the heat, until it is smooth, then remove the pan from the heat and place it in a bowl of ice and water. Continue to beat the mixture until it becomes very thick.

Nut Meringues

Japonais

Ground almonds may be substituted for the ground hazelnuts used here. Ways of assembling these meringues with fillings and icings are shown on page 28.

To make about 50

200 g	hazelnuts, blanched and finely ground	7 oz
10	egg whites	10
300 g	castor sugar	10 oz

Beat the egg whites to stiff peaks with 100 g (3½ oz) of the sugar. Sift the remaining sugar and the ground hazelnuts together and fold them delicately into the egg whites. Using a piping bag with a plain 5 mm (¼ inch) nozzle, pipe the mixture in spirals 2.5 cm (1 inch) in diameter on to silicon paper. Cook the meringues in a preheated 170°C (325°F or Mark 3) oven, with the door slightly open, for about 1 hour or until the meringues are dried out and very slightly golden in colour.

AUGUSTE J. ROULET
LE LIVRE DES FRIANDISES

Buttercream

To make about 600 g (1¼ lb)

5	egg yolks	5
125 g	sugar	4 oz
10 cl	water	3½ fl oz
250 g	butter, softened	8 oz
1 tbsp	strong black coffee, praline powder, liqueur, lemon juice with a little grated rind, or 90 g (3 oz) chocolate melted over hot water	1 tbsp

Whisk the egg yolks until they are thick and foamy and light in colour (about 15 minutes by hand or 7 minutes with an electric beater). Over a medium heat, dissolve the sugar in the water and cook the syrup to the thread stage (*Basics booklet*). Pour the hot syrup into the whisked egg yolks in a thin stream, beating all the time, and continue to beat until the mixture is cool. It will be pale, thick and fluffy.

Cream the butter in a bowl with a wooden spoon until it is smooth, then stir in the whisked egg mixture and beat it with the wooden spoon until all the egg is incorporated and the buttercream is smooth, light in texture and shiny. Stir in the coffee or other chosen flavouring.

Italian Meringue

This meringue is used for lightening fillings and mousses and for piped decorations—on the top of tarts, for example.

To make about 350 g (12 oz)

250 g	sugar	8 oz
10 cl	water	3½ fl oz
4	egg whites, stiffly beaten	4

Dissolve the sugar in the water in a heavy saucepan over a low heat. Bring to the boil and cook the syrup until it reaches the hard-ball stage (*Basics booklet*). Pour the hot syrup in a thin stream on to the beaten egg whites, whisking all the time, and continue whisking until all the syrup has been incorporated and the meringue is very thick and glossy.

Meringue Buttercream

To make about 600 g (1¼ lb)

350 g	Italian meringue mixture (*above*)	12 oz
250 g	butter, softened	8 oz

Cream the butter with a wooden spoon until it is smooth, then beat in the meringue mixture until it is completely incorporated and the buttercream is very smooth and light.

Creamed Cake Batter

This batter is suitable for making the small moulded cakes shown on page 30.

To make about 20 individual cakes or one 25 by 38 cm (10 by 15 inch) cake

125 g	butter, softened	4 oz
125 g	sugar	4 oz
2	eggs	2
125 g	flour	4 oz
1 tsp	baking powder	1 tsp

Beat the butter with a wooden spoon until pale. Cream together the butter and sugar until the mixture is light in colour and fluffy. Add the eggs, one at a time, beating well after each addition. Sift the flour and baking powder together and gradually fold them in with a metal spoon. Butter and flour individual cake moulds or a 25 by 38 cm (10 by 15 inch) shallow baking tin, and fill two-thirds full with the batter. Bake in a preheated 190°C (375°F or Mark 5) oven for 10 to 15 minutes, until golden-brown. The top of the cake should feel springy and the edges shrink away slightly from the sides of the mould or tin. Allow to cool slightly in the moulds or tin before turning out on to wire racks to cool completely.

Cup Cakes

To make about 15

125 g	butter	4 oz
125 g	castor sugar	4 oz
2	eggs, lightly whisked	2
125 g	flour	4 oz
¼ tsp	baking powder	¼ tsp

Cream the butter and sugar thoroughly and beat in the whisked eggs. With the last of the egg, add the flour and baking powder. Divide the mixture among paper baking cases, filling them two-thirds full, and bake them in a preheated 200°C (400°F or Mark 6) oven for 15 minutes. When the cakes are cool, they may be finished by one or more of the following methods:

Butterfly cakes are probably the best known variety. Choose cakes which are quite flat on top and, with a sharp knife, cut a thin slice from the top of each cake. Cut this piece in two. Spread the cake with jam and pipe a generous star of whipped cream in the centre. Replace the two half-slices of cake, butterfly fashion, and dust with icing sugar.

Crown cakes: Again, cut a thin slice from the top of each cake, but this time cut it into four or six even-sized pieces. Spread each cake with jam and pipe a high star of whipped cream in the centre. Then replace the pieces showing the cream in the middle. Decorate with a tiny piece of glacé cherry and dust with icing sugar.

Basket cakes are made by once more removing a slice from the top of each cake. Spread the cake with jam and pipe with whipped cream—rather more generously to one side. Replace the slice at a pretty angle to show off the cream. Finish with a piece of angelica or a glacé cherry and dust with icing sugar.

Cork cakes: Using a small cutter, 1 cm (½ inch) across, cut a cork-shaped piece from the top of each cake. An éclair pipe is ideal for this purpose, while even an apple corer will suffice. Fill the bottom of the cavity with jam, pipe a star of whipped cream on the jam and replace the cork at a rather jaunty angle. Dust with icing sugar.

Iced cup cakes: If there is a little rim of the paper case above the level of the cake then it is a simple matter to ice it with water icing. Make up 60 to 90 g (2 to 3 oz) of icing sugar into water icing by blending it with about 2 teaspoons of water, and, using a teaspoon, run a little over the top of each cake. The paper case will prevent the icing running down the sides and looking messy. Decorate with a silver ball, a glacé cherry and angelica or a piece of walnut.

MARGARET BATES
TALKING ABOUT CAKES WITH AN IRISH AND SCOTTISH ACCENT

Little Almond Cakes

This simple mixture plays tricks in the oven. It is put from a teaspoon into little paper cases and baked. At first it rises but, since there is no flour, it falls again to give a little case of almond mixture suitable for filling. For variety, ground Brazil nuts might be used instead of the ground almonds.

To make 30 to 36

125 g	ground almonds	4 oz
90 g	butter	3 oz
90 g	castor sugar	3 oz
	apricot jam	
	double cream, whipped, and sweetened or flavoured to taste	

Cream the butter and sugar together and gradually work in the ground almonds. Place teaspoonfuls of the mixture into little paper sweet cases. Bake in a preheated 180°C (350°F or Mark 4) oven for 10 to 15 minutes, or until lightly coloured.

When the cakes are cold, peel off the paper cases. Before serving, fill them with a little good-quality apricot jam and pipe with a star of whipped cream.

MARGARET BATES
TALKING ABOUT CAKES WITH AN IRISH AND SCOTTISH ACCENT

Savoy Sponges

Biscottini alla Savoiarda

To make about 48

7	eggs, yolks of 3 separated from whites, whites stiffly beaten	7
325 g	sugar	11 oz
1 tsp	ground cinnamon	1 tsp
300 g	flour, dried in a 150°C (300°F or Mark 2) oven for 15 minutes	10 oz

Beat the four whole eggs and the egg yolks with 300 g (10 oz) of the sugar in a bowl. Add the cinnamon and flour. Combine these ingredients and add the egg whites. Pour the mixture into small buttered tins or paper cases. Sprinkle with the remaining sugar and bake in a preheated 170°C (325°F or Mark 3) oven for about 30 minutes or until the cakes are golden, soft in the middle and dry. When they are cooked, remove them from the tins and serve them plain.

GINO BRUNETTI (EDITOR)
CUCINA MANTOVANA DI PRINCIPI E DI POPOLO

Café Brûlot

A brûlot bowl is a large silver or copper bowl.

To make about ¾ litre (1¼ pints)

½ litre	hot strong coffee	16 fl oz
10 cm	stick cinnamon	4 inch
12	whole cloves	12
2	oranges, rind thinly pared and cut into slivers	2
2	lemons, rind thinly pared and cut into slivers	2
6	sugar cubes	6
¼ litre	brandy	8 fl oz
6 cl	curaçao	2 fl oz

In a brûlot bowl or chafing dish, mash the cinnamon, cloves, orange and lemon rinds and the sugar cubes with a ladle. Add the brandy and curaçao and stir together until the sugar has dissolved. Carefully ignite the brandy. Gradually add the coffee and continue mixing until the flame flickers out. Serve hot in brûlot cups or demitasses.

DEIRDRE STANFORTH (EDITOR)
BRENNAN'S NEW ORLEANS COOKBOOK

Romanian Coffee

Roumunsko Kafe

To make about ½ litre (16 fl oz)

3 tbsp	pulverized coffee	3 tbsp
4 tsp	icing sugar	4 tsp
2 tsp	cocoa powder	2 tsp
½ litre	water	16 fl oz
	vanilla sugar	
	single cream	

Mix the coffee, icing sugar and cocoa powder together in a Turkish coffee pot or a small saucepan and pour on the water. Over a low heat, slowly bring the mixture to just below boiling point, removing the pot from the heat *before* the froth starts to rise. Pour, without straining, into four demitasses or small cups. Serve the vanilla sugar and cream separately so that each person can add them to taste.

DR. ALEXANDER DIMITROV BELORECHKI AND
DR. NIKOLAY ANGELOV DZHELEPOV
OBODRITELNITE PITIETA V NASHIYA DOM

Irish Coffee

The amount of whiskey used depends on the preference of your guests, but generally the ratio is about one part of whiskey to two parts of coffee.

To serve 6

60 cl	hot strong coffee	1 pint
30 g	sugar	1 oz
About 30 cl	Irish whiskey	About ½ pint
	double cream	

You will need six wine glasses with wide bowls. Put about a teaspoonful of sugar into each glass. Pour 3 to 4 tablespoons of Irish whiskey on top of each spoonful of sugar, then pour in the hot coffee to within 1 cm (½ inch) of the glass rims. Stir the coffee, whiskey and sugar gently until the sugar has dissolved. Rest an inverted spoon on the rim of the first glass, so that the bowl just touches the top of the coffee, and slowly pour double cream over the back of the spoon to a thickness of about 5mm (¼ inch). Pour cream into the other five glasses in the same way and serve.

Cardamom Topper

To make about 1.25 litres (2 pints)

1 litre	hot strong coffee	1¾ pints
¼ tsp	ground cardamom	¼ tsp
⅛ tsp	ground mace	⅛ tsp
17.5 cl	double cream	6 fl oz
1 tbsp	sugar	1 tbsp
1 tsp	vanilla extract	1 tsp

Combine the coffee, half the cardamom and all the mace and keep warm over a low heat. Beat the cream, sugar and vanilla extract in a chilled bowl until peaks form. Pour the coffee into cups and top with the whipped cream mixture. Sprinkle the rest of the cardamom on top.

JAN BLEXRUD
A TOAST TO SOBER SPIRITS AND JOYOUS JUICES